THE STORY OF KHAJURAHO

Dr P K Agrawal

MD PUBLICATIONS PVT LTD
NEW DELHI
www.mdppl.com

Published by :

MD Publications Pvt Ltd
"MD House", 11, Darya Ganj,
New Delhi - 110 002
Phone : +91-11-45355555
E-mail : contact@mdppl.com
Website: www.mdppl.com

Photographs by Sagar Agrawal

ISBN: 978-81-7533-332-1

Published and Printed by Mr. Pranav Gupta on behalf of **MD Publications Pvt Ltd** at Times Press, Delhi.

कुमारी सैलजा
Kumari Selja

पर्यटन मंत्री
एवम्
आवास और शहरी गरीबी उपशमन मंत्री
भारत सरकार
परिवहन भवन, नई दिल्ली-110116

Minister of Tourism
and
Minister of Housing & Urban Poverty Alleviation
Government of India
Transport Bhavan, New Delhi-110116

Foreword

The temples of Khajuraho are the World Heritage Site. These were built by the Chandellas. These magnificent temples attract lot of foreign tourists. The temples not only depict amorous couples in stones but also display life in medieval times. There are well meaning carvings of gods and goddesses, warriors, musicians, real and mythical animals, and, of course, the celestial nymphs.

Dr. P.K. Agrawal in his fictional work entitled "The Story of Khajuraho" has unfolded the myth about the legendary union of Hemavati, the local beautiful maiden, with Moon god which is the main story behind the construction of these glorious temples. While narrating the story, Dr. P.K. Agrawal has dwelt on the sculptures of temples and made the construction process very interesting. This book has been written in the backdrop of the Indian ethos and culture.

I don't know what veracity can be attributed to this story from historical point of view, yet someone has come out with his own version. Dr. Agrawal has done his job well because he comes from the same Bundelkhand region.

Dr. P.K. Agrawal is a public-spirited writer. I am sure that this book will be welcomed by all those who are interested in knowing the background of the intricate art and architecture of these temples which are pride of India.

Selja

(Kumari Selja)

Transport Bhawan
New Delhi

Preface

Khajuraho is a wonder of mystic sex in stone. The temples at Khajuraho are more than a millennium old. The antiquity has not reduced their beauty but has been adding grandeur and importance day by day. The pleasures in life have been engraved on the stone panels of the Khajuraho temples so thoroughly that these figures absorb the visitor for a while and take him to some other world of fancy and excitement. The erotic images are unique features of the sculpture of Khajuraho. But there is a deep meaning of each carving at Khajuraho co-related with the Hindu pantheon and the Indian ethos and culture.

As a person coming from the land of Chandellas, I tried to weave the local supporting juicy legends of history into a story. It is an interesting story. The beautiful maiden Hemavati had the union with the Moon to save her father Maniram from the royal punishment for his astronomical error. Her brave son Chandravarman laid the foundation of the Chandella empire. The successive kings continued to build temples at Khajuraho as their religious and cultured capital. However construction and architecture of important and representative temples only could be discussed in this work to continue the web of the story. The temples pay silent tribute to the love between Hemavati and the Moon.

These temples stand alone and preach love, beauty and tenderness to the world community. Tourists visit these temples as the best sex-destination in the world. But sex is the tip of the iceberg of the sculpture of Khajuraho.

Every visitor whether the Indian or foreigner is wonder

struck after the visit of Khajuraho. This work is to satisfy his curiosity regarding ambit of construction of temples at Khajuraho.

'The Story of Khajuraho' is lucid and interesting. It entertains the readers profusely. I now, don't want to come in between the story and the reader which will unfold as freely as the art form at Khujuraho.

I am very grateful to Mr. Pranav Gupta, Director of MD Publications Pvt Ltd, New Delhi, for his kind cooperation and support for this book.

Dr P K Agrawal

Contents

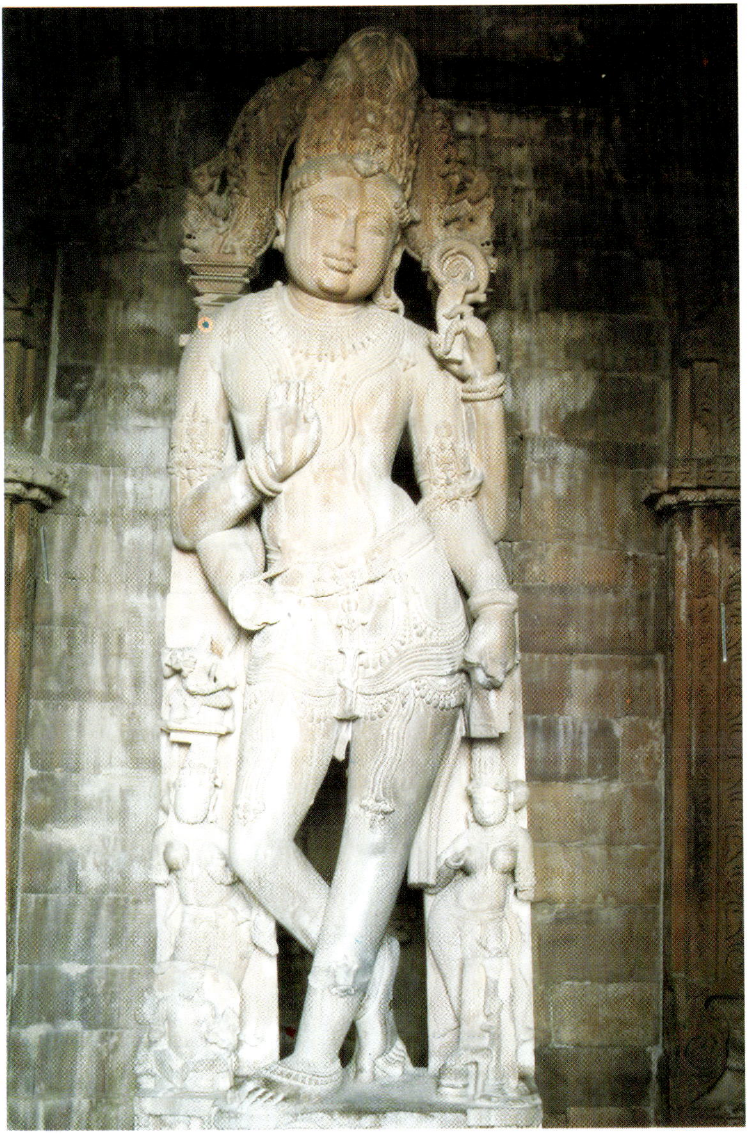

VISHNU

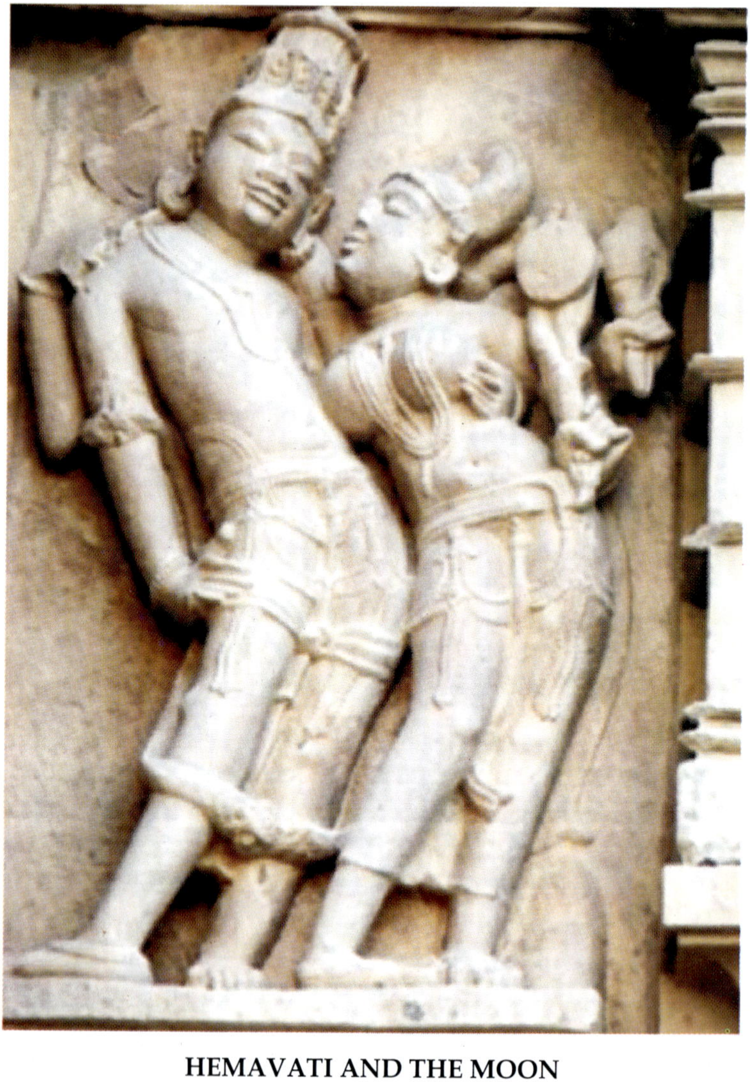

HEMAVATI AND THE MOON

1

Meeting of Hemavati and the Moon

Standing on the stairs of the Rati tank the widowed young daughter of Maniram, the royal priest of Kalinjar prayed to the Moon, "Oh Moongod ! My father has committed an error in calculating the movements of stars. As a result, the particular night Purnamasi (full moon night) has been declared as a full dark night (Amavasya). Is it such a blunder that all the honour of one family will be destroyed? The king and the people around him are forgetting the great sacrifice my father has made for the kingdom and the royal family after his migration from Varanasi. We are being so much condemned and cursed that if the full dark night doesn't convert into full moon night, my father will take trance into the water. We will have to follow the father. Who else will look after me and my mother after his death? I know that my father has lost all connections with his native family in Varanasi and my maternal uncle in Kalinjar will not accept us due to social boycott. Is one bonafide mistake in astronomical calculation so severely punishable?

Oh Moongod ! Save my father and our family from dishonour and death. I still want to enjoy life which was cut short due to sudden death of my very young husband whose union has left unforgettable imprints on my body and in my mind.

Oh handsome Moongod ! You are the only person who can save us. Please save. I am prepared to do everything to save my father and family."

There was a whisper from the sky in her ears, "Oh beautiful Hemavati ! You are the most beautiful woman on earth and in heaven. None can turn back from your deer eyes. No one can take away his eyes from your beautiful body. Oh Lady ! Don't tempt me. You don't know what you are offering to me. Nobody on earth and heaven can say you 'No'. I have never changed the full dark night into full moon light. It will amount playing with normal functioning of the universe. This universe is running smoothly because everyone is performing his assigned dharma or duty in a proper way. Do you like that this universe should stop for you? I am also bound by my own duty cast upon me by the Almighty. According to cycle of nature, it is not possible to change the dark night into the moonlight. I am also accountable to Vishnu, the maintainer of this universe. An infraction of discipline on my part may invite wrath of Lord Shankar (the destroyer) on me

You ponder over again and let me know finally.

Hemavati said, "Oh ! Moongod ! I have neither patience nor time. Time is fast slipping out. My father has to go before the king to account for his mistake tomorrow. I know only two persons in this world i.e. my father and my mother. I don't want to listen anithing else except the conversion of dark night into moonlight night by hooks or crooks. I have lost my dear love. I don't want to loose my father again. I shall be alone in this world. This world will not allow me to live peacefully. My beauty will be my arch enemy. I am, therefroe, prepared to make any sacrifice. I have given this promise to my father that I will save him at all costs. He did not believe in me. How could his ordinary daughter do a miracle? Seeing him disheartened and dejected, my conviction has hardened like a rock. A conviction in mind is more important than the promise made in open. If I do not accomplish this, how can I stand before myself? This body is not as valuable as self".

The Moongod said, "If you are determined, I shall come down on earth and fulfil your promise. I shall then have to

manage the whole cycle. But I shall not go back empty har
Dear Hemavati ! Be ready. You will have to satisfy me".

Without thinking for a moment, the rosy lady said, "Oh! Moongod!! come I am in wait for you and all your desires will be fulfilled".

The Moongod descended on earth in an unusual manner. With his gradual descent, the earth started getting lightened, darkness started disappearing and glittering started spreading in all four directions.

It was the summer night. The breeze was blowing which was filling the atmosphere with passion. As breeze became more fierce, the lotus in the water came around the feet of Hemavati. The trees of teak, Salai, Khair, Bamboo were making noise as if they were welcoming unusual light even on Amavasya day. The breeze was so strong that Hemavati was unable to keep her clothes intact on her body. The clothes were either flying alongwith the air or were sticking to her body where they should not stick. Hemavati was very elated and excited that she took a dip in water. Being drenched, she could hardly control her beauty exposed in the open.

On her own, she was thanking the Moongod and was spellbound thinking that father will be spared by the king and his courtiers because there was light on Amavasya and hence father's forecast was factually correct.

As she was lost in the ideas of her success, the Moongod was in front of her with all his handsomeness and grandeur. Hemavati was bewildered. She could never dream that there could be a man so handsome, fair, healthy and lovable on earth. As she opened her eyes, she found herself in intense love with Moongod. She fell for him. She forgot the past and decided to go with him. Her lifelong desire was going to be fulfilled. She prostrated before the Moongod. Lifting her magnetic body and embracing her, the Moon said, "Darling! Your position is not in my feet, it is in my heart. You are my love. I cannot live without you. When I saw you from the heaven, you are much more beautiful ! I wish that you stay in my eyes so that I can ever see you with my untiring eyes. Drink to me only with thine eyes and I will pledge with mine. Whatever sacrifice I have done for you that is nothing compared to your grace. If I take you to my abode in heaven, the nymphs in heaven will be jealous of you. I feel that I have done a right thing coming down to you. Now, all bonds are broken. Forget that I am superior to you. We are two souls in one body. Come and embrace me. Be one with me".

Holding hand of Moon in her hand, Hemavati proceeded to a desolated place where shrubs of karonda,, panwar, thuar and baikal had spread the carpet on the uneven earth. While holding, touching and walking, Hemavati murmured to Moon, "The Dearest ! You are my life. I want to give you all that I have. I am your chattel and I want to give it to you. You are my savior and avenue of good life. You are my present and the future. We are two in one. There is neither body nor any person in between us. I am elated to have you. My lasting desire is fulfilled. I sacrifice myself for you. You may have many but for me, you are the only one. How can I describe my mind to you that I want to give best of mine to you."

Both of them were not knowing where they were heading to. But they were heading towards a destination from where no man or woman likes to return.

While proceeding unmindful, the saree of Hemavati got entangled into a shrub, and it slipped from the upper portion. The Moon found the beauty standing openly in front of him. He could not control himself. While trying to disengage her saree from shrubs, the Moon embraced Hemavati times and again and she equally obliged him by kissing him time and again and hugged his gracious body time and again. They were so engulfed in kissing and hugging that they forgot where they were standing. Hemavati murmured, "The trees of Amaltas and the date palms are gazing our activities." Saying this, Hemavati blushed.

The Moon said, "I am also feeling guilty conscious as my subordinate stars are eyeing as to what their boss is indulging in. But I am bold enough to accept your love and there is nothing to hide. I can not remove my eyes from your lotus eyes, your intoxicating body with attractive curves. I have in deep passion for you. My eyes are not satisfied. There are many maidens who have offered their hands to me but for some valuable return. I have lost my heart in your love. Your unselfish love and sacrifice are unparalled. I can not afford to be away for a moment from you. You don't feel that you are my nymph. You are my heart. In fact, I am of you and I am for you. You give me elixir of life and make this earth the heaven."

The twenty one year old love lorn heroin was not able to support herself due to the weight of her bosom and buttocks and gave her hand to the Moon to step forward. Passion had overtaken her senses. The atmosphere was full of fragrance of full blown lotuses of the lake, flowers of ketki and intoxicating breeze of kadamb trees and date palm trees. The parrots had gone to their nests after their meeting noises with their companions after daylong toil in search of food. Cuckooes were still filling the air with their sweet songs. Loud cooing of the doves was causing the breeze sweet though summer had caused all the desolation and destruction. Had the God not created night specially during summer, the human being would have gone mad.

Hemavati was walking with the Moon towards the hutment on their plot of land made for guarding their farm. As there was no crop, there was nothing to guard. In fact none can guard one in her own hut. Perhaps the hutment was eagerly waiting for the celestial guest alongwith the earthly beauty. Inspite of their all efforts, they could walk slowly as both were in deep passionate condition. The heavenly incense used by the Moon and the lotus fragrance in Hemavati were causing them talking in their eyes more than walking physically. Being unmindful, the serpent like hairs of Hemavati got netted in a palm tree. The Moon playing the role of the man had a trying time to get her hairs unetted. In the meleee, Hemavati surrendered fully to the Moon. The Moon virtually lifted Hemavati bodily and brought to the hutment. The Moon first took out his ornaments, crown and small weapon. Hemavati's clothes were already torn and were just wrapped on her body like a creeper on the trunk of a sandal tree. The Moon proposed, "My Beloved !! I have come for you from all the way from heaven. Make our meeting an ever memorable one".

Hemavati like a drunken person responded "My Lord !! Have I even for a moment refused any advance from your side? You are my man I dreamt of and wish for. You can do whatever you like. Woman surrenders after lot of thinking. But once, she surrenders, she has the courage to accept her love in front of the world. This Hemavati of yours has been thirsty for mating for years after the death of my first love. Can Hemavati expect a better suitor than you? My ambition is fulfilled by your first sight. My only prayer is that you don't abandon me after love. Where shall I go? I shall have no shelter. Your bold chest, powerful arms and all pervading handsomeness are my greatest shelter. Don't forget this poor Hemavati. If you do it, the earthly women will never believe in heavenly guests. The Moon replied, "Dearest lady !! I am pinning head down in your love. Give me your love. I am not able to understand what you say. I am blind in your love and an immersed in your beauty. Let us be two in one. Then everything else will follow".

The hutment was getting pleasant light from the Moon himself. The atmosphere was full of love and passion. There was none around except exciting nature. Both were at the climax of passion. There was no cause to pause. Hema disrobed herself. Hema and Moon became two in one in few moments and continued so until both became unconscious. The Moon regained consciousness faster and left the scene with a message on the wall of hut by a piece of coal, "Sorry, I have lot of things to do." Hemavati regained consciousness after a while as she has still been enjoying elixir of life. Her long thirst was quenched by heavenly wine in place of water. When she regained consciousness, she found everything lost for her. She only found the writing on wall. But she had no more time at her disposal. She adjusted her clothes and body though it was an uphill task for her to do that. She prepared herself to go to her father who by this time had returned home from the king's palace. Her goal was achieved though she lost something personal in the process.

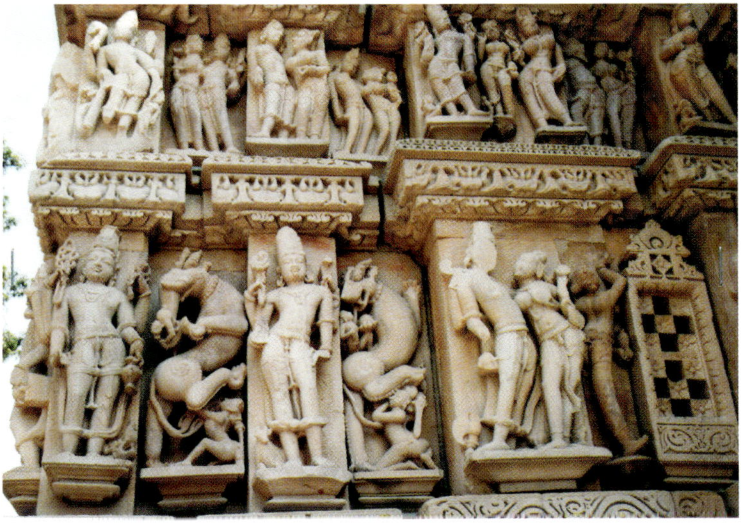

LOVE IN VARIOUS FORMS

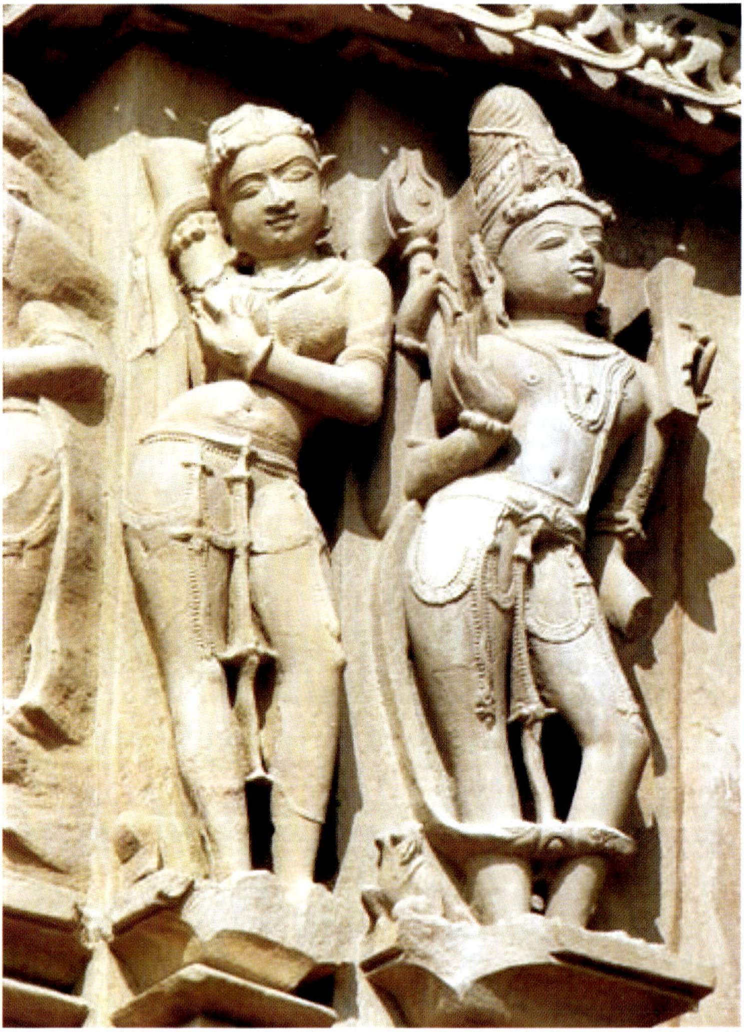

LOST IN LOVE

2

Hemavati's Love Message through the Clouds

In her somber condition, Hemavati appeared before her parents in her house. To her great satisfaction, she found her father delivering one sided dialogue to her mother. Both of them were so much engrossed in the story that they did not stare at her daughter who had occasioned that to happen. She noticed her father so happy as he was happy on the occasion of becoming the chief priest or 'purohit' of Kalinjar king and on the occasion of her kanyadan i.e. giving her hand in marriage to her minor husband.

Hemavati forgot what she had just lost in sudden disappearance of her paramour, the Moon. She attentively heard her father Maniram describing the proceedings of the king's court.

The King: "Prime Minister! What punishment has been decided to be given to Maniram for wrong calculation of the Amavasya night i.e., the last day of the dark half of the month?"

Prime Minister : "My Lord! Maniram has achieved a miracle which none could achieve on the earth so far. Today's 'Amavasya' has been converted into 'Purnamasi' and we see light everywhere, which is more than the normal 'purnamasi' which comes once in a month. We have two 'purnamasi' this month due to great miracle by our Chief Priest Maniram."

Ministers, courtiers and other audience who were present in the royal court or 'durbar' agreed with the Prime Minister and raised their hands in support.

The Queen: "Oh king! I am also astonished to find a great miracle of nature today at this juncture of time which none could calculate or anticipate except our reverend chief priest for which we should suitably award him rather punish him".

The King: "Remove the curtain and let me see the miracle of Maniram".

Long curtains of the court hall were removed and everybody present in the public witnessed the great miracle of nature. The light at that time was so glittering which should be at least thrice of what is generally watched on full moon night. Secondly, it was so pleasant everywhere which people of Kalinjar had never experienced before.

The King : "I agree with all of you. I did not even imagine that all this could happen. From now onwards, Maniram will continue our undisputed Chief Priest for life. I announce one hundred one gold coins and hundred one acres of land in the honour of venerable Maniram for his knowledge of astrology and astronomy. On the other hand, his opponents are exiled from the kingdom of Kalinjar."

Maniram: "Oh king! I am a Brahman. A Brahman is for welfare of all. A priest has to be unmoved in success and failure. He should treat his foe and friend alike. Therefore, I request you to grant them reprieve and allow them to live in his Excellency's kingdom. I so request your Honour".

The king granted the request of Maniram and gave reprieve to the opponents of Maniram. Hemavati didn't want to lessen the enthusiasm and pleasure of her father whom she adored more than anybody in this world. She didn't want to tell him in what return he had got that victory. One honour was acquired but another honour was lost in return. Her father kept on saying, " This is the day when my ancestors in the heaven must be proud of this Maniram who has done a miracle inspite of living in a distant place from the religious and cultural capital of the country. Our other relatives in Kashi should feel diminutive and jealous that they could do nothing sort of this miracle. They have lived always on mercy of successive kings and on alms received from their patrons."

Mani Ram was thus roaming and roaring around with the flag of victory in his neighbourhood. He specially visited those people who had underestimated him and castigated him whenever opportunity came handy to them. Mani Ram said " See. This neighbourer of yours has done such a wonder which was never done on earth and will never be done again. You must have heard about moon eclipse but not the conversion of the ' amavasya' into ' purnamasi'. Gaze from your naked eyes before it disappears. Everyone around was waiting for hanging of Maniram today. But Maniram got the highest award from the king of Kalinjar." I have got one hundred one acre of land at Khajuraho where I shall peacefully settle and die. Today, our neighbourhood has come in the limelight in the entire Bharatvarsa. Is it not a thing of great pride and merry making for all of us?" beaming Maniram said.

The neighbourers were at loggerhead with Maniram and his family because Hemavati didn't give any space to many suitors in the locality. But neighbourers had no alternative but to digest the glory of Maniram which was unheard of. Everybody thought that as an impossible task. Maniram accomplished that and returned home victorious. He went in sleep with golden dreams that he had won the 'Aswamedha Yajna' i.e., he had won the world.

The night was slowly getting dark and was assuming its natural self. The women are suspicious of other women and can understand other women very easily specially in matters of sex, pregnancy or other emotional matters. Mother of Hemavati asked Hemavati, " Dear daughter! I suppose that everything is right with you. I don't find you in normal self. Your dress is unsettled. It is torn in few places. You are uneasy. I hope that nothing objectionable has happened with you, Nothing inauspicious lies under your disquiet. I have never seen you for all these twenty one years in this abnormal condition. Your father, as you know has never paid much heed to my suggestions. He is only concerned about his performance as the Chief Priest, proceedings in the king's court or queen's conversation with him. He has no time to stay and stare at us."

Hemavati replied, " Mother! Father has given all that in the house which a man should give for his family. We have no problem in leading a decent and respectful life. The last obstacle is also over. In return, we have got lot of gold coins and sufficient land to shift from this obnoxious neighbourhood. I don't know whether people of Kalinjar have ever accepted your marriage with the father. Now, they are up in arms against me and like to grab me and my honour. The Father is a simpleton. He knows his idols and his family and the king. He has no fourth concern in the world. We should support him with all our capacity and resources." Hema's mother did not feel good at Hemavati's comments about her husband and retorted, " Do you mean that I didn't sacrifice for his sake. I have even dissociated at times from my own parental family who are so conservative. Have I committed any lapse in your upbringing? "Had I not fully devoted and looked after you every moment, you would not have grown in such a beautiful woman. I have kept your sorrow of losing your ex-husband miles away from you by engaging you in more fruitful activities. I am proud of you, Hema!" Seeing tears in her mother's eyes, Hemavati could not explode the bomb which she had hidden in her womb.

Days passed, yet Hamavati could not dare expose the blunder she had committed before her mother.

Her mother often said to her, "Hema, why is that you are never to your normal self? You are lost somewhere, sometimes you don't respond to my calls which was not the case earlier. Sometimes you keep on gazing outside. As the night descends, you become more introvert. Sometimes, you even don't recognize the presence of your dear father."

As they were talking, Maniram came inside the house and the talk between two was interrupted.

Hemavati didn't have many friends around because her movements outside the home were restricted due to her gorgeous beauty which was flowering day by day like the growing moon of moonlight fortnight. Whosoever looked at her, he or she was just spellbound to see her speckless grandeur of beauty which created passion for her. But none was there to share her thoughts which were constantly bothering her. Ultimately, she found that it is cloud and cloud only who could take her message to her paramour. She prayed to the cloud", "Oh cloud! You are the closest to my paramour. You are situated in the sky and he is beyond the sky. You are the only one who can reach him. You are very sportive. You move with the winds. Therefore, you can do this feat for me. I understand that the Moon, my love is very busy and I found him very scared of Lord Shiva, yet you can convince him that he may keep me with him in his abode in heaven. Tell him that I can't live without him for a moment. I shall not disturb him in his work which he performs as a true 'karmayogi' during day and night. I shall on the other hand be supportive in performance of his duties or dharma. I shall perform my job as his better half. You are just like my brother. I am sure you will be able to transport me to him. You carry so much water. As compared to that, my weight is nothing. Brother! Help! Your sister is in distress."

The cloud said, 'Oh Hemavati! You are labouring under a misconception. These gods in heaven are surrounded by luxuries and nymphs. They forget every other thing. There is dazzling music, dancing, joking, dining and merry making going on. You know that the Moon-god is very simple and good-hearted person. He is one of the best gods in heaven. Therefore, people don't realize his strength and valour. He is the greatest of all.

He is even more powerful and useful than the Sun. Though he doesn't have his own light and is lighted by the Sun, yet if he is not there the whole world will be reduced to ashes. None will be able to work what to say to relax and sleep. He has life in his heart whereas the Sun is only vomitting rays of light and energy. Who can tolerate the thrust of sun if the moon is not there? It is the rumour perforated in the sky that the night, he had descended to consummate marriage with you, he had given his responsibility to his subordinate. Due to his mishandling, there was a disturbance in the meditation of Durvasha saint who complained this matter first to Lord Shiva who assured him to look into the matter personally and assured the saint to punish the Moon if he was found guilty. Then only the Moon could be saved of the curse of sage Durvasha who is synonymous to anger in the world. Lord Shiva enquired into the matter personally and he arrived at the conclusion that the Moon had not done justice with you. He could have sent the Moon to the earth to live with you as per demand of justice of Lord Shiva who does equity with everyone. Yet he found that the universe wouldstop if he punished. the Moon without making alternative arrangement. He could not find suitable substitute of the Moon. He ultimately thought it proper to warn the Moon and gave him a black spot on his face so that he would not misuse his charm and handsomeness to exploit earthly maids and others. Hearing this, Hemavati was stunned. She became unconscious. When she regained consciousness, she found that the cloud was not there. She murmured, "The Moon is all in all for me" She wished, "I don't want my paramour to come to me. Let him be there. If he is happy, I am happy. I am not so selfish as to cause embarrassment to my love. I can live in the memory of that night for whole of my remaining life. I am happy that he is working for the good of this universe. After all, it is I who invited him to save my father. Well-being of many is more important than the well-being of a single person. After all, he has left his precious gift with me which I shall cherish for the remaining part of my life. I pray to Lord Shiva to excuse both of us and bless us so that we become a happy love' lorne pair like Krishna and Radha. So it be. But Oh cloud! You keep on coming at least after every summer so that I can at least talk to my paramour through you."

It was the month of July. It had not rained for last two years. This year was the year of rains. Thanking the cloud messenger. Hemavati said, " Oh cloud brother! I am happy that you have arrived at the call of your poor sister and have taken all the people of Kalinjar out of nervous and agony of drought. Their hearts have are smiling alongwith the dry grass and leaves of plants and trees at your auspicious arrival. People have started singing and dancing in your honour. But I am no longer able to control the release of my pent-up passion. You take some time out. Go to my dear one and bring me his news. Insist on my behalf that at least, he should pay a brief visit during this season of lovers. If he doesn't come down during lover's season, I shall be angry with him and curse him. You are not only a mix of vapour, smoke, water and wind, you are the embodiment of life. You are the ablest messenger of lovers. I am sure that you will be welcomed by my beloved. He will offer you the best hospitality. Your news of hospitality will keep me lively until you arrive and thereafter. You are so powerful that even the bravest and the noisiest on this earth are scared of you. When your roar, it is like a great elephant nuzzling. You float above the highest mountain Everest. You are the greatest and the mightiest. I know that you have also to obey Indra like my dear Moon has to follow Lord Shiva. But before the orders by god Indra are issued to you, you will be able to accomplish my mission and come back. The airgod is always with you like it stood by our side during adversities. He will stand by you in all adversities. I am also praying to the 'Airgod' so that it takes special case of you during your journey to the abode of my paramour and back. It is just possible that you may not have interview with my Moon, yet the fact, you visited him, will give me lot of solace and happiness. I shall enjoy fragrance of his abode and body through you as carrier. I am not able to bear his separation any longer. Do something, please." She exclaimed, "Oh beloved! I am lighted by yours light like the soul is lighted by God. I am your wife like the soul to God. I am nothing without you. Remove darkness from my heart and soul."

The cloud flew to the Moon in desperation even fearing rebuff by him. The cloud messenger found to his pleasant surprise that though many big wigs were waiting for seeking instructions or blessings from the Moon, yet he gave hearing to the poor and meek cloud messenger from Hamavati. The Moon understanding the message from Hemavati said to the cloud messenger. "Oh cloud! Tell Hemavati that I love her as much as she loves me. But love is not something on which a person or the world can sustain for all the time. We have to sacrifice our love for the greater good of the humanity, the flora and the fauna. Tell her to be happy. Our offspring will be the king. He will be a mighty ruler in the world and from him many branches will spread out in all directions. He will do something wonderful which will make our love memorable in all times to come. You will be able to live happily with this memorable reputation.. He will construct pilgrimage monuments for all the passionate lovers of the world like us. I shall duly look after him. But let our love he a secret one. True love is in giving and giving constantly."

The cloud messenger returned with lot of enthusiasm & radiance reflected on its face. The cloud emptied all its stock on Hemavati and in turn, the whole locality was benefitted due to the benediction of the cloud messengers. Nobody knew in Kalinjar why abnormal events were happening in Kalinjar and around. Booty of nature was raining on Kalinjar. In the thirsty lands of Jajakabhukti, it was raining cats and dogs. None knew about the second wonder by Hemavati. It was bestowed upon Kalinjar by Hemavati's associates. As per advice of his so called cloud brother, Hemavati decided to keep her love quite secret. Hemavati exclaimed, "Oh! Lover!! I am always yours. Whatever treasure I have, you are my source. I am thankful for being united with you. My mind is always at you like the 'chetak' bird who looks at the cloud with one and only concentration and devotion to send its message to her love. I have taken in everything from you but I couldn't give any thing to you in return. Due to my insistence, you have been punished by Lord Shiva. For that I am very sorry and insist you to forget the black chapter at the earliest. I was very fortunate to have your benign love. I have everlasting longing for it. I am never tired in your love. You are the

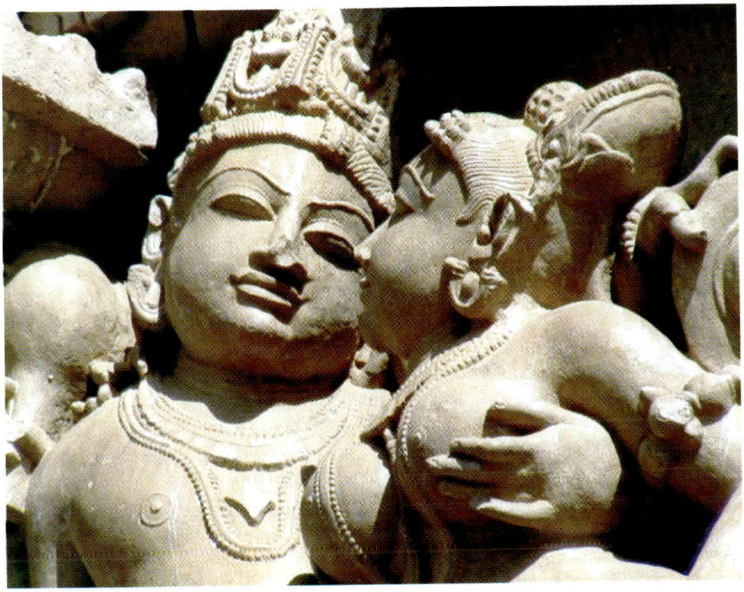

MEMORIES OF UNION

treasure of all qualities. I am ashamed to be always selfish. I am so selfish to have you always with me. What can I do? In every of my action, I find your reflection. In every thought of mine, you appear from nowhere. Sometimes your meeting appears suddenly like the lightning and makes me immobile. I am lost in that thought. I then have no desire to work or to eat. I only want to be lost in your sweet memories. You didn't look at my faults and gave me all your love. In return, I could n't even say 'good bye' to you. I am extremely ashamed and sorry. You tell me how I can pay back for this. I am prepared to undergo any penance. But you and only you can come to my rescue and show me the way out. Come again."

The Moon said, "Darling Hemavati! I have been revolving around the earth unstopped for ages. Your love and heavenly beauty stopped me only once in my constant journey. Those moments were like years for me while I could stay and stare. You had neither committed any blunder nor you had overstepped in my life. It was I who in fact enjoyed your love to my full satisfaction. I always see your face reflected in my mind and my eyes are always thirsty and longing to see you again. I can never forget our meeting. It appears time and again. But my 'dharma' prevents me from any more digression. Yours was a selfless love which I shall always cherish and stand by you and by the side of the coming guest as a symbol of our union. He will have a glory like me in the world which will be ever satisfying for you. This will be the magic result of our love. You are the only mistress of my mind. Physically I may not be able to be with you, but I am always there with you with my unseen form. Nobody else can occupy your place in my life. Henceforth, whatever love I shall distribute, that will be the extension of your love. I am always for you. Don't feel that you are lonely and helpless. I always repent on what I had done to you. Forget it and pardon my offence. Keep on giving your pious love to me so that we may be hailed as true valorous and great lovers."

Hemavati got emotionally broken after listening to her paramour, the Moon. That awakened her in sleep and she realized that all those were dreams while she was talking to her lover. Life is also like a dream. There are persons in the world who convert these dreams into reality through their consistency, perseverance and hard work.

3

Ballads of Separation of Hemavati

Hemawati could no longer hide the secret of the fateful night from her mother. Her body started glowing with the aura of the moon. She started vomitting. Luckily vomitting occurred when her father was away at the place to worship the family deity of the Gaharwar ruler, Inderjit. Hemavati summoned courage enough to disclose to her mother that she had consummated 'Gandharva' or temporary marriage with the Moongod to save the life of her father on that fateful night. Though she saved the honour of the family, yet in the process she sacrified her honour.

Her mother said, "Hemawati, this is the real loss of honour of the family. The chastity of the woman in the family is the honour of the family. Wars have been fought to preserve the chastity of the woman. Many families have been destroyed on the issue of sanctity of woman. Therefore, Hemavati, you should have no doubt that you committed a grave blunder by surrendering to the Moon. Your father could have managed something on that date. These are royal issues which are very complex and can be tackled by way of intelligent handling. I have never seen in my life that somebody so close to the King's family, has been banished from the Kingdom or hanged. I was sure that same solution would emerge out as we are pious, people and your father had committed a bonafide error." Hemavati regretfully said, "My respected mother! If you don't support me in my adventure, I shall have no other alternative but to give up my life. Pardon me, my mother. I could not come up to your expectations. What I thought to be the greatest sacrifice, has been termed as the greatest blunder by you. What a folly committed by me?"

Saying this, Hemavati started sobbing. Consoling her, mother said, "Hema, don't worry. Parents pardon their children for faults. I shall always stand by you. Don't think of committing suicide. It is the greatest sin in life. None has the right to take one's life. As life is given by God, He only can take it back. Now you will be responsible for two lives. I shall take care of your child. What is destined, can't be changed. This is what a grand mother always dreams of. I had taken for granted that I shall never become the grand mother. I thought that I would be deprived of that greatest happiness for an old lady because of our strict traditional values. But don't be excited. We have to conceal this from your father at all costs. He will never be able to digest this information. His reaction will be fierce and detrimental to all of us. One should tell the truth but the truth should not be so offensive as it can kill the other person. After sometime, I shall shift you to Asu with your maternal uncle. None will be able to know anything about the incident. By the time, your pregnancy will not be able to be concealed, I shall shift you to the farmland at Khajjarpura. There, you will be able to give birth to your child, grow him up and then your father will be duly informed about the episode. Don't bother. I shall take care of every thing. You only do what I say. From today, you are not only by daughter, you are also my friend or companion. You have to be very careful during this stage of pregnancy". Hemavati took complete refuse under the able guardianship of her mother. She replied, "I shall do whatever you ask me to do.".

For the change, Hemavati was shifted to the maternal uncle's home at Asu village. There she had nothing to do except to talk to her lover. She would often lose herself in memories of her encounter with the Moon and brood over for hours. She would recreate the same incident time and again

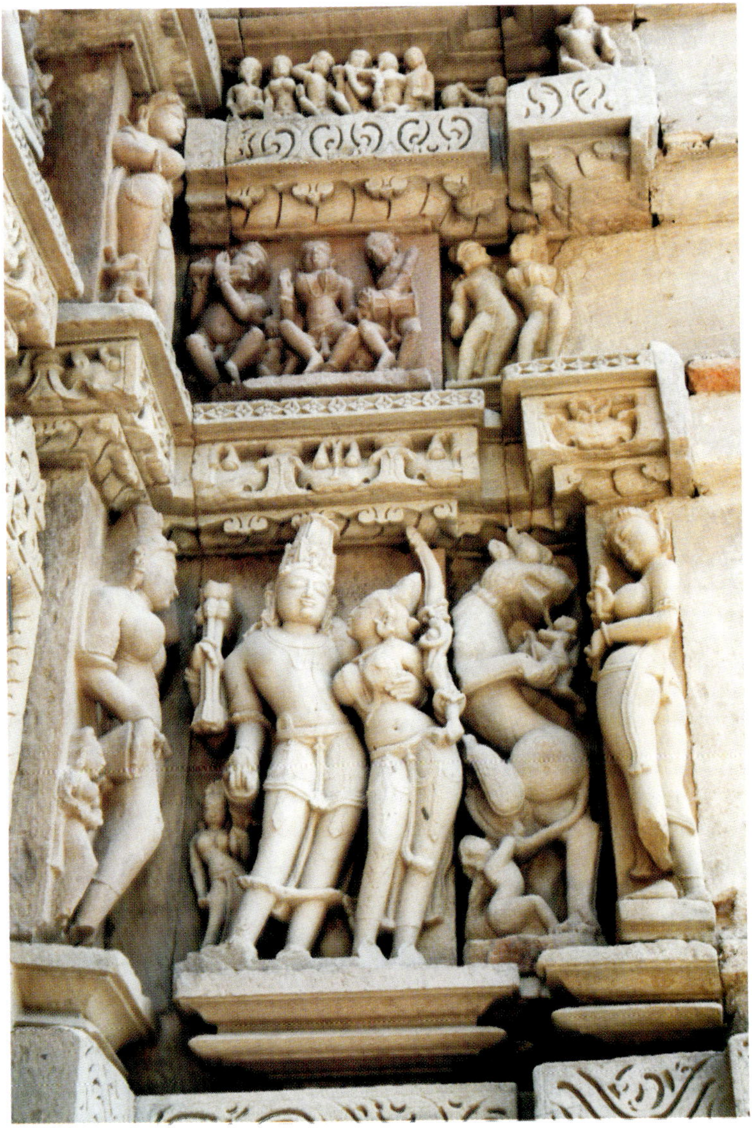

MESSAGE OF LOVE IN STONES

like the nest of sand on the sea shore and would enjoy. She often recalled, "Alas! I would not have committed that blunder. My love! Either you accept or kill me. Due to your eclipse, I get dejected. How long can I keep on staring at you? On that night, we became one soul in two bodies. How can then I stay away from my bigger soul?" The Moon replied, "Hema, you need not waste your time and energy to gaze at me. You have a precious gift of mine. Your best love to me will be to preserve and further beautify my gift. Devote whole heartedly to this."

Hemavati said, "Oh Lover! Don't snatch my right to be lost in your memories. I shall now have your real love in separation inspite of it being union of suffering. In your union, every suffering is acceptable to me. I don't know my passion has become more intense in separation than the one on that fateful night."

The Moon replied, angriy, "Dear Hemavati, enough is enough. I have given you all that required for your comfortable and reputed living on earth. My peers in heaven crack jokes on my visit to earth. It is unbearable. Don't came to me time and again. Learn to live on your own.

Enough is enough. My job is not a play between man & woman. I have given you powerful shelter of Chandra and wealth of the Kalinjar kingdom. The temples to be built by you and Chandra will keep you alive in the annals of the world history. What else a person on earth be?"

Hearing reply, Hemavati, broke down and started weeping. While weeping, she uttered, "My dear, don't be angry and upset. I shall live on your memories. I don't need any other thing from you. But don't snatch my memories."

Hemavati wondering in his memories said to Moon, "My beloved! You are all powerful. You create tide in the vast sea. Human body is more water than any thing else. Thus, you control two-third of this earth. You are the light to the travellers in desert. You make light available to all birds and animals in this universe. Their habitat is lighted by you and you alone during night. Whatever light is produced and used by the whole mankind is just the tip of iceberg of your light. You are our life. My mind and body is one with you. During moonlight fortnight my mind is also full of zeal, energy and happiness whereas during dark fortnight it goes into indifference and despair. Why are you afraid of Shiva and Vishnu? Come down and embrace me once more. I am praying Shiva and Vishnu that they will not censor your visit to earth again. I am sure that they will listen to my prayer as Lord Shiva is a very kind god. I shall not request you again. Please have one more final real meeting so that I can express my love to you. First meeting was during my unconsciousness."

Getting no further reply from her lover, Hemavati recalled the cloud messenger and said, "Oh brother cloud! You are my only resort and help. You convey my message to my lover daily at least in lovely rainy season because I well know that after this season, even you will not be available at call to me. Therefore with your help on, let me enjoy every day of these four months. My passion is also high. So help me. Take my message to my lover and bring back the message at the earliest whatever cryptic it may be. Even your arrival upto the gate of my lover or touching his body or the walls of his bed room and back will suffice. That will refresh me time and again. I wish you a good luck for your great journey. I don't want that you should be unfortunate like me. You should always remain united with your mate, the lightning and should never be separated from her".

Hemavati was glowing in beauty so much that she had become a problem to her maternal uncle's house. Her lips had become reddish like plum and her eyes like those of a deer. Her buttocks had become so heavy that her walking was slowed. Her breasts became too heavy for her to stoop slightly.

Hemavati was conscious of her georgeous beauty, but she decided to have one pointed aim i.e. to look after the gift of her second and final paramour. Throbbing in soliloquy, she thought, "This World is very cruel. I see no hope for my fondest wish to meet my lover. My lover is so busy with his better half Rohini that he has no time even to take my message and reply. But none including my paramour can dictate to my dreams. I am happy in this loneliness yet the hearsay about me often create bubbles of unhappiness to me and to my shelterer. Have I done such a crime that I don't have six feet long and three & half feet broad place to live in this world? If this public criticism continues here, I shall request the Moon to curse my critics. It is because I have to reap the consequences of some wrongdoing on my part in my previous birth."

Hemavati was passing her days feeding her womb. She found a good companion in the maternal uncle's house. His recently married daughter Prabha had returned from her husband's house after a brief sojourn with her newly wed husband. Both were placed in a similar situation. Prabha suggested Hemavati, "Hemavati, you are very lucky. Actually, first night is all in all. After that, even sex becomes routine. Therefore, whatever you have enjoyed, is the ultimate goal of each couple. We are not able to meet so frequently due to family commitments and values. All the elders ask us to give them a gift of a son which you have become successful. Hema! You have achieved the goal of a amorous couple."

Hemavati said, "This love is also amorphous. I know how much I love him but I don't know whether he loves me too. If he doesn't reciprocate, my love goes on and on...... I am happy in your company. At least I can share my happiness and woes. My mother has pushed me fearing adverse reaction in our neighbourhood". Prabha said to Hemavati, "Keep your union and feelings secret. I shall also keep all these things quite secret. Tell here that your husband has gone to Kashi to study Vedas and other rituals otherwise society will eat into your vitals."

Hemavati agreed that her advice was fantastic and everyone would believe in. Hemavati would often say to her new companion, "That was the fantastic moonlight night. Any woman can be proud of being with the Moon who is the most handsome person in this universe. I found him equally so sweet and powerful that I can not imagine a better man than him. I just fully surrendered myself on that fateful encounter. No body is to be blamed. It is I and only I who is to be blamed. My thirst for sex is to be blamed. I shall cherish that memory for rest of my life and live on that. He called me his 'chandra mukhi' as if, I had the face as beautiful as of him. He promised me to take to his world of heaven. I was so lost in him that I don't remember what else he kept on telling me. I rather became lifeless during the meeting. I could not talk nor hear. I wish that every woman sometime has that kind of experience."

Prabha said, "Hema! I also enjoyed my first night. My husband is equally a muscle man and handsome. Over and above, he is a good person. He is very considerate. But he doesn't spare me during night. I also like your think that one night is enough for a woman to live on. I only remember that. I forget subsequent meetings. I don't know why? Do you not remember your first night with your social husband?"

Hemavati said, "Every marriage is followed by first night for confirmation of marriage. I also had the first night with my first husband. But that time, we were not so mature in the art of sex. So it was so-so. It can in no way, be compared with the grand finale ".

Thus, both friends would indulge in all sorts of dirty conversation about their sexual life which can not be revealed to anybody else. When women start talking dirt, none can surpass them.

Hemavati used to be so much engrossed with her new friend that she could not spare time to talk to other members of the family. As a result, the male members of the family i.e. her maternal uncle and his son Suresh decided not to further bear the burden for giving her shelter in their house. She could clearly feel it and often expressed her feeling to Prabha. "Is it a wrong on the part of a woman to be beautiful? Everyone wants to talk to her and if she talks back, the man understands that she likes him. If she doesn't talk or keeps indifferent then they say that she is proudy. Further male folk become inimical to her and try to harm her. Where will a beautiful woman go? Is it a curse to be beautiful?" Prabha consoled her and said, "Beauty and sex in every organ of woman keep this world revolving around her. Otherwise who would care for us? We shall be like any other animal or bird. None will care unless one cries like a child. Our beauty is in itself an achievement. These bloody men toil and earn for day long to enjoy the woman's beauty during night. We have to be very cautious. Specially women like you should keep balance by showing close to everybody specially men and also by keeping equi-distant from everybody so that struggle doesn't flare up among competitive men for us. It is just like walking on the sword. Thus woman's birth is considered inauspicious in our families. We shall make our life as the best and most enjoyable." "Friend! Forget it. Let us go out in the open and enjoy beauty of the nature. We shall prove that two women can love each other and can be better lovers than a man and a woman."

Both of them often went out in the winter afternoon to their farms. The fields were blooming with wheat, barleys, cauliflower, cabbage, pea, tomatoes, brinjal etc. There, they found women working with small weeding hooks to take out unwanted grass obstructing in the growth of plants. There were sparsely located continuous fields of mustard which looked like yellow carpets laid around on the ground. The yellow mustard plants were dancing slowly and slowly as if they were lost in the memory of their lovers."

Prabha commented, "We are lucky that we have not to work in the field. We are privileged because we are young and beautiful. This is a premium for beauty. Let us thank to the Almighty who has structured us so. Many other women you see here, are just women in gender. They have to work just like men."

Hema said, "Don't bring other working women in our talk. Our talk is privy to ourselves. I am lost and jealous of group of yellow mustard plants who are enjoying the memory of their love. I really sometime feel why my lover has made my breast like cabbage. I am not able to support my body or beauty whatever you may call it. My breasts have lost softness and are bulging to declare my love. In the background of yellow sarees of mustard flowers spread around, the fragrance of jasmine makes me intoxicated. But I don't have my lover around. What can I do? My lover is not so easily available. You are the only one available here. Help me." Saying this, both of them kissed each other and then they separated immediately fearing eyes of working women.

Prabha said, "Yes, I can also see that even the best of lining of your blouse is not able to support and shelter your bosom from others' eyes. Your undergarment is not able to hide your bulging buttocks and golden colour of your skin."

Both the fiends returned back to the home before dusk after enjoying grown up yet soft peas from plants in the field.

The pregnancy of Hemavati was developing like the moonlight half of the lunar month. Everybody was asking the maternal uncle of Hemavati as to when her husband would return to Hemavati. He had no answer. None was prepared to listen that he was in Kashi for studies. Traditionally, husbands are around when women are pregnant. He was feeling socially insulted.

At the same time, Maniram, the father of Hemavati was unable to bear the volley of questions or doubts regarding disappearance of Hemavati. Everybody was interested about the whereabout of Hemavati, whether he or she was related to her or not. Poor Maniram was not apprised of the full facts by his loyal wife fearing his dangerous reaction. But sin can not be hidden for long. One day, it is to come out. It is to account for.

Hemavati's mother Sona had been continuously advising Maniram to leave Kalinjar palace and settle at Khajuraho in the vast tract of land gifted to them by the king. Maniram agreed partly and they started building small cottages there on the farm so that they would go and settle there peacefully. Sona was sure that she would not be able to conceal facts from Maniram for long. Already, people were becoming restless. The air was venting high with rumours. Common people of Kalinjar were gradually denoting the miracle as some artificial creation by Hemavati. Maniram was not able to convince even a single person around him. That was making him quite tense. He would often boil down on the poor wife and fire her, "Why do you not tell me the truth? After Hemavati is born, she has become a problem to us. Firstly, her beauty killed her first husband. Now, she is killing me. Where is she? I like to kill her and end our problems. When will she return? What will I reply to so many mouths?"

Sona replied, "I told you as many times that she is at her maternal uncle's house. She is well threre. I can tell you that she has not committed any crime that you want to try her in your court. I have safeguarded her from her childhood. I shall continue to protect her even at the cost of my life. Parents are for children. What is the meaning of our life without Hemavati? Future generations will laugh on us that we could not even shelter one beautiful girl. Let God give me strength to pass this crucial test. Let God protect Hema and bestow on her all happiness."

Unable to bear the burnt of anger of husband Maniram, Sona sent for her brother. The obedient younger brother obliged the sister without delay. They had conference and decided not to disclose truth to Maniram at any cost. Sona and her brother were examined and cross-examined by Maniram for hours together time and again but truth was not disclosed to him. Being fed up, Maniram said, "Both of you are one and the same."

Sona's brother said, "Sister! You are like Goddess to me. You had cherished me in place of the mother. Time has come to discharge my debt to you. I shall do whatever you say to do." Both sister and brother went into deep consultation and after long deliberation, it was decided that Hemavati would be shifted to a hamlet on Kanvati river where an expert nurse resided for delivery of the child. She was well known to the brother and it would be a smooth delivery without any tension to anybody including Hemavati.

Sona's younger brother explained to his sister, "I have a

friend after crossing river Ken in Khajraim. It is a tiny village where my friend Chintamani Vaishya dwells. He has no child. He will fully take care of her. One expert tribal nurse resides there. She is flawless. She has magic in her hand. Each delivery by her is safe and smooth. The newly born will be perfectly normal. Allow me to take the decision. When you shift to Khajuraho, I shall send Hemavati to you and keep her newly born child with us for sometime. The problem is to keep Hemavati due to her fierce attraction. There is no problem to keep her son. After you convince or reconcile my great brother-in-law, I shall produce her great son who will be the one and only one in the Aryavarta or India. I think that our plan is O.K. Let us pray God that we become successful in our plan which is the best in the given situation and has the sanction of 'dharma' or duty".

Sona started weeping before her brother which only strengthened her brother's resolve to protect Hemavati and her child upto the last. A brother can not withstand the tears of his married sister especially the elder one.

As per the plan, Hemavati was shifted to an unknown surrounding. Chintamani Vaishya was a good and considerate person and had a happy family life. His wife was chaste like Savitri fully devoted to her husband. Both of them had won the heart of each dweller of the tiny village. Though he made lot of profits in his small grocery shop where he sold goods in exchange of foodgrains, none condemned him as he was always helpful to everyone in distress. He himself was the Ayurvedic physician and could treat the villagers for seasonal ailments through local herbs or home made medicinal products. He had learnt to administer injections and could give some well-known western treatments.

Hemavati was astonished to find herself in a new house. She was happy that she was away from the public glare, wild comments and criticism and was under day-night supervision by a doctor which she required most in that condition. The local nurse was called in. Her one touch to the inflated body of Hemavati gave her so much soothing effect that she forgot everything else and started enjoying her pregnancy. All pangs of pregnancy disappeared as her beloved disappeared on the rise of the sun. The nurse declared, "Hema! You will be the mother of the greatest child on this earth. My lifetime ambition will be fulfilled because such a child will be born by my hands before my death. For that, I am grateful more than what you will be grateful to me."

Chintamani was also feeling happy that he would be a part of the great incident in his small house. He advised Hemavati, "Be cautious and happy now-a-days. This the most important period for the unborn child. He is listening what you are listening. He is thinking whatever you are thinking. Your thoughts and actions will make immortal imprints on its mind."

Hemavati pondered, "I have become a fugitive due to my beauty. What else is my fault? It is because of my sheer effort to save my father's life, I invoked the Moon-god and then every thing else followed. It changed the world for me. It reshaped my destiny. This was my pride for beauty which steered me to venture upon the said adventure.

Had I agreed upon to marry one of the simpleton in the locality, I would have enjoyed so many nights like Prabha. None would have criticized me. My husband would have been obliged throughout my life time after enjoying my beauty. He would have served me like a serf. Now, there is no going back. The great always behave in an ususual manner. So at present, none looks at me. Therefore, there is no problem. How shall I survive when one will not look at me after some years? Perhaps I shall have to survive as a mother only. I am like the Ken river whose water or stream can never return back inspite all residents of Khajraim desiring it to flow back."

She would for hours gaze at the flowing water of Ken and sing the following song;

"Oh Ken! Why do you flow?
Why do you flow so slowly and calmly?
Don't you feel enthusiasm or turbulance?
For whom are you flowing?

I know you will continue flowing
I shall also keep on flowing like you."

Life is like the flow of the river. She was looked after well by the pious wife of Chintamani who derived celestial pleasure in serving others. She was a symbol of purity, sacrifice and cordiality in the tiny village. She was fully contended in herself. She had no issue, yet she was happy. Hemavati got lot of inspiration from her last leg of shelter. She often got engrossed in thoughts of her future, "How shall I pass the rest of my life without any support from the institutional husband? How shall I pass my day to day life without talking to anybody? I cannot talk to my mother and father for a long time.

After all, social norms are to be maintained with them. Without social norms society will disintegrate. I shall have to survive by talking to my kid only.

She got a happy news that their farm house at Khajuraho had become ready and her mother Sona was likely to shift there soon. She was happy with the idea to live with her family at Khajuraho away from the public glare.

Winter has gone, spring has just arrived. The mango trees were in full bloom. They were as heavy as Hemavati. Even the black berry trees were full of violet and black colour fruits. The atmosphere was buzzing with the traditional rite of offerings to the god of love with songs and dances. She also offered her love to her beloved Moon in following verse;

Oh my beloved! Sometimes you are shining
Whereas sometimes you go behind the light.
Sometimes you play hide and seek
With my my cloud messenger.
Sometime you give hopes whereas
Sometimes you only give despair.
Though all of your shapes are also worshipped.
Sometimes, your black spots are clearly visible.

Sometimes you are as bright as the sun.

You are sweetish whereas the sun is cruel.

You offers us to wait for lover whereas the sun always asks us to work.

I wish you always be full moon shining for your Hemavati."

Thus, she was always lost in thoughts of her lover.

On the day and time fixed, she delivered a healthy and stout boy child shining as the Moon in the house of Chintamani on the bank of the Ken river.

4

Birth of Chandravarman

On hearing the child's birth from Hemavati, her mother Sona rushed to Khajraim and asked her brother to bring Hemavati to her new abode. He at once proceeded to Chintamani's house but the village head nurse refused to allow the mother and the newly born boy to move before fifteen days. Sona was becoming restless to see her grand son but she had no other way except to wait for sometime.

She applied all her energy and resources to set the place in order so that Hemavati could take rest for few months. Her brother even agreed to keep the newly born in his house but neither Hemavati liked the idea nor the child would have stayed without the mother as it knew only Hemavati on the earth.

Sona persuaded one of the female farm workers to take care of Hemavati and her son.

Hemavati came to Khajuraho with her shining son. Her mother embraced both of them for hours and thanked God for successful delivery. She welcomed the new guest in her family in a traditional way with conch sound and flowers. She was with them for ten days and then decided to join Maniram.

Reaching Kalinjar, she found that hearsay, was doing rounds that Hemavati had given birth to a male child. She found it an uphill task to deny the fact. Before the matters went out of control and Maniram was expelled from the kingdom, Sona suggested to Maniram, "You seem to be tired. You are not able to perform daily routine of worship happily. God will be angry with such type of indifferent worshipping. Time is ripe now to resign from the taxing and controversial job of the head priest and take up comparatively lighter job as priest of Lord Shiva's temple at Khajuraho."

Though Maniram used to shout at Sona as matter of right now and then, yet he used to give maximum heed to her advice and suggestions. Ultimately docile and devoted wife used to prevail upon the harsh and strict husband. He also found that a conspiracy was being hatched against him by the ambitious priest with the patronage of the Prime Minister in whose bungalow he was serving the idols. The king had almost given all the management to his Prime Minister and was himself busy in merry-making. Maniram said to Sona, "Don't' worry. At an appropriate opportunity, I shall leave the job so that it might look that I have left on my volition. Land at Khajuraho is sufficient to support us during the remainder of our age."

Sona got permission of Maniram to go to Khajuraho for three months to set right the land and start cultivation there.

Sona reached Kharuraho and became closet with her grandson and named him Chandraverman. She exclaimed, "These are the happiest moments of my life! He is my greatest refuge! I get lost in him and forget rebuke of my husband. My love is as pure as water of the Ganges. It is as selfless as the emission of rays by the Sun. Let God give me strength to live and embrace my grandson upto the last moment of my life."

Hemavati wished that the desire of her mother would be fulfilled. She was happy that she would be discharging her obligation towards her mother after her sacrifice for her father.

Hemavati and Sona were looking after Chandravarman more than anything else. Her mother forgot about the farm and cultivation whereas Hemavati even lost sight of her beautiful body. On few days, she even forgot to stand before the mirror and to look at her gorgeous body. She hardly

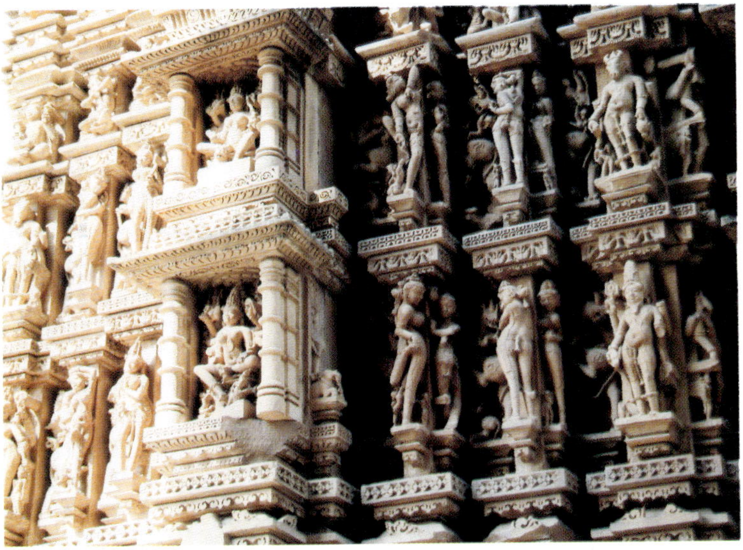

LIFE AT KHAJURAHO

remembered her paramour in the presence of Chandravarman. Maternal grandmother Sona and the farm labourer cum maid Ramkali were looking after Chandravarman who was nicknamed as Chandra or Chanda. Ramkali called the child as Chanda whereas the grandy called him Chandra.

Both of them ensured that Chandra had stabilized in its health. However, Chandra had become quite naughty getting unfettered love and unquestionable patronage from the grandy. Sona left Khajuraho after three months giving charge of Chandraverman to Ramkali. Sona said to Ramkali, "You look after the baby like me. I should not hear any complaint. I should find on my return that my Chandra had grown stronger & valiant. I have to look after your Baboo ji. I don't know how he is facing public after lot of rumour about Hemavati in the neighbourhood. He is very simple person but is very sensitive to the public opinion. I really don't know where it will end. I fear that it may destroy happiness of our small harmonious family."

Ramkali said to Sona, "Maaji! I don't know why you people care so much about public. My husband doesn't bother at all what other say about us. He drinks and creates scenes in the street. He is even now going ahead producing children at the rate of one every year. I cann't resist him. If I resist, he beats me up. The last one is very weak. I even can't feed him my milk. I am very much worried."

Sona left for Kalinjar. At Khajuraho farm house, Ramkali made Hemavati free of worries about Chandravarman. When Chandra cried very much, Ramkali would even feed her milk to him in the absence of Hemavati. It was not possible for Hemavati alone to fulfil the need of milk feed of the stout son Chandra.

Both were happy that Chandravarman was growing into a child which was not seen earlier on earth by them.

Hemavati was sometimes lost in the thoughts of her lover, the Moon and would think heartily for the marvellous gift he had given to her for which she was very much proud of. Her heart moved with the waves of moon. She rocked with the moon.

The monsoon arrived at and clouds started gathering in the sky. Seeing clouds, Hemavati remembered her lover. She had no other go except to invite the cloud messenger through these words –

Oh cloud! You are in bits and pieces,
Sometimes you are white,
Sometimes you are black,
Sometimes you change colours so fast,
That can not be described in words.
You form rainbow which is marvel of nature.
But that too is for some time.
Sometimes, you are fierceful,
Sometimes you are quiet like mouse,
Sometimes you are as thin as jasmine creeper,
Sometimes you are as big as the big banyan tree,
Sometimes you are near the heaven,
Sometimes you touch the mortal beings,
Sometimes you bring rains,
Sometimes you bring only fear,
Sometimes you bring despair,
Sometimes you breach your promises and disappear,
But sometimes you pour water.
You drink water from sea and rivers, and kiss the mountain peaks,
Sometimes you form the reddish dark sunset,
Whereas sometimes you share the morning glory of the Sun.

I pray that you never be away from my sight. When people around Hemavati found that she was engrossed with clouds, none disturbed her. She used to take time to come to the normal self. After all, everybody has to realize the reality of life and engage oneself in daily chores of activities to keep the cycle of this world moving.

Maniram often quarrelled with his wife Sona on some

small issue or the other. He said, "Sona! All of you have ganged against me. I have no news of Hemavati. I don't know whether she is still alive in the world or has died. I don't know whether somebody has kidnapped her and killed her. You people don't bother to update me about her. I don't know how my Hema is whom I had grown with so much love and care which nobody on the earth can give. You are doing some conspiracy against me. I hear so many incoherent stories about Hemavati from public that I am ashamed and distressed. How much shall I tolerate? It is becoming unbearable to me in this age. Some people even say that she has given birth to a bastard. Some say that she has eloped with her paramour. Some other say that she is staying in illicit relations with somebody. These hearsay are slowly reaching upto the king. I find that my prestige has gone down in the eyes of our patron and my peers. I can not stay in such a hostile atmosphere at Kalinjar. It is all due to you." Saying this he angrily threw the food plates in front of him. This is the greatest insult to a housewife in India.

Reacting sharply, Sona said to Maniram, "You have known me well during these long twenty five years of our wedlock. You know how I served you during all odds. After seven rounds around the fire during marriage, I stood by you like a rock. When you fell in love for me, I abandoned my family and came with you thinking that our life would be happy. But you are making my life hell by firing me continuously for the past few months for the incidents over which I have no control. All these things have happened because myself and our daughter stood by your side in all ups and downs. It is very easy to be angry on somebody who is weaker than you. Can you show your red eyes to your patron or peers? This is the life of a woman. She has to struggle throughout her life. That is my fate. That is my destiny. I accept it as it is. None is to be blamed for such an impasse except myself. I must have committed sins, in my earlier birth. Therefore, I have to live to see this day. God! Why don't you lift me from this earth?"

Saying this, Sona started weeping. Seeing tears in her eyes, Maniram diluted himself and became defensive.

He said to Sona, "Why do you weep? Tears will not solve any problem. Let us sit down and make a plan for the future peacefully. Whatever has happened, we have to face jointly. We have to live or die together."

No wife can accept word of death from her husband. Sona also became desperate. Both sat down and decided that by next month, Maniram would resign and get relieved from the job of the chief priest and the family would finally shift to Khajuraho. By that time, Sona will go to Khajuraho and arrange everything in Khajuraho so that Maniram will have no problem to settle down at the new place.

Sona came back to Khajuraho. She advised Hemavati and Ramkali to make a nice setting for Hemavati's father to return to the place.

On seeing Chandravarman, Sona got lost in love of her grandson. It was growing so nicely that anybody on earth could be happy and proud to see it.

Hemavati also started attending to Chandravarman more vigorously because she was told by her mother that only way to make her father happy was to satisfy him with the exceptional qualities of Chandravarman. Otherwise, all their peace and happiness would disappear in the sea of anger of Maniram.

Forgoing all her love for the Moon, Hemavati devoted to teach Chandraverman the art of fighting and made him walk on his own here and there so that he would become a stronger person than the king of Kalinjar.

On being told how Maniram was publicly condemned, mother and daughter decided to make Chandravarman so brave that he could overthrow the king of Kalinjar and shut the mouth of public for ever. Both of them thus got engaged to achieve one point goal to make Chandravarman the axis of their ambition. In their pursuit, Ramkali was the willing and able help.

Ramkali's husband said, "What are three women doing for one child all the time? Our children have grown up without any support. You don't have little time for me. How can a woman live without man?" Ramkali angrily said to her husband, "I have given you more company than required. You have treated me like your kept. I was earning but was sleeping under you. You were only drinking and enjoying life. Who will support so many children? I know you will not share my job. But a mother can't eat without first feeding her children. Now I shall have to work like a donkey. Therefore, I have decided to help Didi Hema and mother Sona to make Chandravarman the king of Kalinjar so that my dark days will disappear and I shall die peacefully. I want to witness the experiment that to reproduce a lion is better than to reproduce a dozen of jackals." Three ladies thus, got engrossed together in their mission.

Chandra was given bow and arrow, spear and other weapons as toys. These were registering slowly in the nascent mind of Chandra rather than rose, lotus and jasmine flowers. Hemavati had earmarked loneliness for refreshing her love memory. In front of the child, she always presented a brave and caring face.

Sona fully enjoyed her sojourn of last six months at Khajuraho because she well knew that her husband Maniram would not be able to withstand the story of Hemavati with the Moon-god as he was a highly moralistic and conservative person. Her remaining age would be passed to reconcile Maniram and to tolerate his dissatisfaction and anger. She planted marigold, lotus, jasmine, dahlia, chrysanthemums, begonia, zenia and all varities of roses because Maniram had lot of love for flowers. If he could find sufficient good flowers to offer in his daily worship, half day would pass peacefully. She ensured that at least one lotus is grown everyday so that her husband gets one lotus flower to offer to his Lord Shiva. She made it a point that one small pond was always filled with water in their vast farm and its water was never used for irrigation purpose. There were clear instructions in this regard. Maniram's anger will not entertain any logic of economy or practicality.

Marigold was in many varieties from the yellow colour to the dark red, from pigmy size to the giant size. The rows of marigold were growing as if the cultivation of marigold was being done on the farm. Rose (rosaceal) locally know 'gulab' was grown in all available varieties. Rose is the king of Indian gardens. One can not imagine a group of flowers without the leader rose. It has tolerable fragrance alongwith appealing colours red, orange, white, yellow even black. But red one is preferably offered to Gods. Therefore, it was grown in many rows. Actually, other colours specially black one is as a result of hybrid varieties crossed with hybrid teas, like Chandra was born. Unfortunately, the modern rose is losing its characteristic fragrance due to diseases like black spot and dia-back due to its association with the Persian yellow parents.

Jasmine was another variety of flower, locally known as 'Bela' or 'Mogra' so that its strong and sweeping fragrance might keep away Maniram from disturbing the world of Hemavati, Sona & Ramkali alongwith Chandra. It is low-growing evergreen shrub and a climber both, with almost sessile leaves having wavy margins. It is a creeper with simple smooth leaves or mostly with three small leaflets. The flowers are white and borne in many flowered clusters.

Having grown variety of flowers and stabilized child Chandra, Sona started for her journey to Kalinjar to bring back her rebel husband Maniram to Khajuraho.

Things had little subsided at Kalingar yet both of them decided to go to Khajuraho in normal course. Maniram said, "It is better to leave a job with respect rather than leave it in disgust as an unwanted person. We shall get some gift from the king and also shall get a gaddi or post at Khajuraho with full state honour."

On the appropriate day Maniram expressed his final desire to his chief patron, the Prime Minister to the King, "Sir, I want to go and settle down at Khajuraho. I keep very busy from morning to night in worshipping at your place and in the palace. Now I want to meditate and pray for myself so that I may be free from the cycle of death and birth or at least I may secure a good place in heaven after death. Please allow me to leave the job and settle at Khajuraho."

The Prime Minister of the King was a clever person. He advised the king, "It is better to release Maniram at his volition and request. We shall also be free from all the controversies making rounds against him and his daughter. This is in the best interests of the administration and Maniram that he leaves his job with honour." King at once accepted the advice of his Prime Minister as he was looking for an alibi to get rid of Maniram. He said, "Oh Prime Minister! I hardly disagree with you. Let it be approved as you like. However, give some gifts of gold coins and jagir (land) to Maniram so that none can say that this kingdom doesn't care for its retired people who have served the kingdom loyally and obediently throughout their active life."

Maniram got a fitting farewell. He got additional twenty five acres of land near the town Khajuraho and lot of wealth including gold coins, diamonds etc. so that he could build a castle to live in style for rest of his life.

Maniram alongwith his wife Sona was taken from Kalinjar to Khajuraho in a carriage drawn by four horses and was temporarily accommodated in the king's guest house at Khajuraho. Sona got some more breathing time.

Maniram and Sona settled down in their new well-built abode of the king at Khajuraho. Maniram became quite busy in taking over the charge of the Lord Shiva temple from the outgoing priest who was thrown away from the job to accommodate Maniram, the head priest of the king. It was a trying time for Maniram but he had no other choice as he had come to Khajuraho as per his choice. Khajuraho was a deserted place and it was not a cake walk for Maniram like in the palace at Kalinjar. Maniram struggled for almost three months to take charge of the temple including its assets and wealth and next three months to organize worship as per royal rituals. The construction of his new castle near the temple started because his farm house was quite far off from the temple and it was not possible to offer three times prayers in the temple regularly.

Maniram soon became popular for his new rituals of worship of the temple. His predecessor had developed a habit of hemp smoking. He was also having a bad company of some hermits and some youths. The local people were very unhappy with him as because he was spoiling some young boys of the locality. Maniram had all good habits except two. He was very impatient and was unpredictable. Secondly, he was vocal moralist which very few people liked.

As Maniram got settled at the new place of duty, Sona started telling him gradually and slowly the truth of the story of Chandravarman. Maniram always reacted saying, "Why did you not disclose this earlier? After all our Hemavati sacrificed her chastity for my sake. How could I be so ungrateful to her? Gratefulness is a virtue well-established by our scriptures. This one virtue can take a person to heaven."

Sona said to her husband, "I can not afford to take a slightest risk with your temper. Any shock or outburst by you in this age would be fatal for you and for me. I was afraid that you would not be able to assimilate this truth. Then our world would collapse. I assure you that Chandravarman will make you happy. At present, he is grouping with children of his age like Lord Krishna. He will very soon rule over Khajuraho."

Maniram said, "Everything need not be told to the wife. Things keep on happening in the palace. There are intrigues, conspiracies and jealousies yet all die out at one point of time. I suppose that my error of judgement would have been also passed into oblivion with passage of time after meeting some temporary punishment. I can not withstand or accept that Hemavati had invoked the Moon-god for this purpose. However, I am happy so far public doesn't remind me about this incident time and again and I have not to face public censure for this incident. You know well that I am very susceptible to public criticism. I feel that due to me, our ancestors and family have been condemned. Sona interjected, "But you keep on repeating from the Bhagwadgita that one should not bother about public praise or public criticism." "That is the difference between preaching and actual practice. We peach many things but when these things come to us, we became disturbed", said Maniram.

Sona was reassured in herself that there is no worry about the life of Maniram due to the news of birth of Chandra from Hemavati. She therefore, devoted her full attention to Chandravarman without shifting him and Hemavati elsewhere away from her. Maniram also didn't insist. He had virtually no time to spare from the daily routine of prayers and rituals of worship of Lord Shiva.

5

Victory over Kalinjar

Chandravarman had grown and crossed ten years of age. Everybody observed him as a very energetic boy with lot of confidence and leadership qualities. He was hardly interested in worshipping instead, he was interested in wrestling and weapon practice. He won the hearts of local maids and local parents. He increased his group to about one hundred boys who were prepared to do and die at his single call. His great quality was that he never allowed any of his associates to feel as inferior to him. His only mission or message was, "United we win, divided we fall." His message spread in nearby areas of Khajuraho. People in the neighbouring areas under Kalinjar were already disgusted with the king whose men were doing excessive revenue collection by adopting forcible measures.

On the other hand, the king administration took no developmental activities. The people had faced one drought already without any assistance from their king. They were already agitated over the fact that the king had been spending lot of money on his seragtio (harem). He had already forcibly imprisoned two or three Brahman's girls to his female apartment in his palace. As a result all the 'Brahmans' of the regime went against him. He started coming drunk even in Durbar-hall during his cabinet meeting. He even abused his prime minister one day under intoxication. Being aggrieved, the prime minister told to his close colleagues of the cabinet, "I am loyal to the kingdom and its people. Welfare of people of Kalinjar is my only and only goal. Whosoever high king may be, if he obstructs in my mission, I shall bite him like cobra and finish him. Service of people is the only thing which will defend us in long run."

The kingdom was losing income fast as the king hardly went to the town and villages to meet his public and ask them to pay revenue voluntarily. Secondly, the expenditure was increasing day by day.

Chandravarman organized small army of young boys. But the army was without any arms. Hearing that the diamonds are found in mines at nearby Panna, Chandravarman took a trip to Panna alongwith his five most trusted lieutenants. He successfully recruited about one hundred supporters from Panna alone, who assured him sufficient support in the form of diamonds which were mined around Panna and other jewels. Chandravarman returned satisfied with the plan of raising an army of able bodied youths of similar thinking.

Chandravarman had grown to the age of fifteen years. None could overlook him at Khajuraho. He became the uncrowned king of Khajuraho. Maniram reconciled and was happy with the rising moon of his family. The status of Maniram became as grand father of the king which he had never imagined.

Chandravarman, thereafter decided to take on the king at Kalinjar indirectly. He firstly returned the king's summon by refusing to pay revenue imposed on his farm house saying, "It is a grant from the king. Therefore, it is not taxable."

The king's servants did not agree to this. They had to raise revenue by hooks or crooks to save their service. They insulted Maniram. In return, Chandravarman and his associates beat them up heavily. They returned to Kalinjar in a beleaguered condition. The king had no answer. He asked his commander to bring to books the newly rising star of the kingdom.

In the meantime, one leopard had entered the village of Khajuraho and surrounding areas and was causing havoc. It

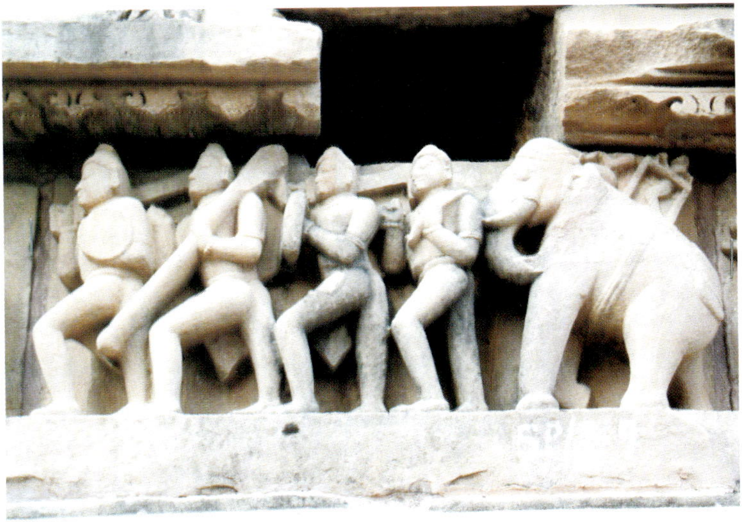

MARCHING ARMY

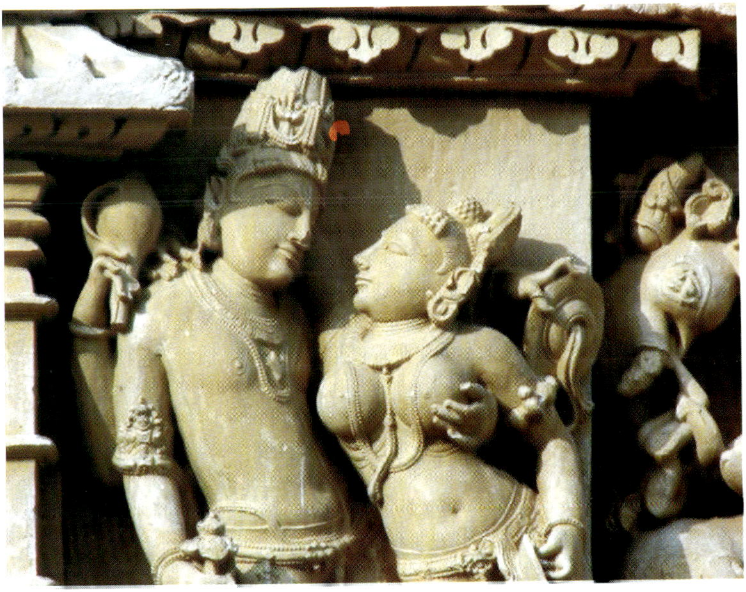

LUST

had already killed two honey and date gatherers and one tribal woman who used to visit forest to collect woodlots and dry leaves. It had broken its teeth during hunting. Therefore, it sprayed itself into human habitation to prey domestic animals and eat crops. One day, it came trekking a bull near a cattle-shed of a farmer. The cattle-shed was closed and therefore, it was waiting in between the cattle-shed and the house of the farmer. The cattle started crying seeing the leopard. Chandravarman was informed by the villagers. He at once went with spears and swords on the spot alongwith five of his accomplices. Chandravarman climbed up the top of roof of the house and took up a position. His associates also took positions on the ground at two places. The leopard is an intelligent and clever animal. Seeing its death in front, it jumped over Chandravarman. Before Chandravarman could throw his spear, it had already attacked his hand of spear. However, Chandravarman attacked the leopard with sword in the other hand and cut its neck. Seeing the animal dead, a large crowd came closer to the leopard but Chandravarman warned them and asked his associates to come up and remove the body of the leopard.

This news spread around like the wildfire. Chandravarman became their undisputed hero. He was taken in a procession in Khajuraho alongwith the dead leopard as a hero. He won the people's heart and trust. He was treated for his injuries in the bout by the local doctor. He got well soon but not without firing by his mother, grand mother and Maniram. Maniram advised him, "We are 'Brahmans'. We need not show much courage and valour. This is the job of Kshatriyas, the warriors. Our job is to pray, read scriptures, spread knowledge and then be one with the God." Chandravarman replied, "But I have to take revenge against Kshatriyas to have insulted you and compelled you to migrate to Khajuraho for no fault of yours except one astronomical calculation error which even the most experts in this field can commit. Allow me to be Kshatriya to take revenge for the injustice done against you and our family like Parasuram. This injustice has made us fugitive in our own homeland.

Maniram said to Chandra, "You do one thing. Build such monumentous temples that everybody will remember me and our family." "I will do that. The aim of my life is to fulfil your unfulfilled desires. But this is not possible without grabbing the kingdom from the tyrannical king. Royal palace has all the wealth."

Maniram felt relieved on that day. There was somebody who was caring so much for him. He forgot the story of Hemavati also, how she begot Chandravarman. He asked Chandravarman, "Do something so that our people who are embracing the Buddhism, come back to our Hinduism. If it continues, Hindus will be reduced to minority in their own motherland." "I promise to do that also," Chandravarman said to Maniram.

Thus, the aims and objects of the mission of Chandravarman got well defined. He started consolidating his army. Necessary wealth to support the raising and maintenance of the small army started flowing in from nearby Panna. Chandravarman himself became busy in strategic matters. He entrusted management of money to his chief assistant.

Moon was the symbol of passion for Hemavati, whereas it was a symbol of pride and recognition for Maniram who saw a future king of his family in the young and innocent eyes of Chandravarman. Maniram gave the following esoteric formula to Chandravarman;

Indians are great fighters,

The world knows so nicely

Honour of India cannot be destroyed.

And steps shall not be retracted at any cost.

This became the secret incantation to the bright, energetic and brave Chandravarman who vowed to abide by it.

Chandravarman with his associates at Khajuraho got manufactured many types of arms of iron. Iron was locally available and they had to bring some manufacturers from outside. They got swords, spades, spears etc. ready. He alongwith his friends practised on targets everyday. He also practised wrestling and local martial art regularly, so that none in his group could beat him. He thus, became an undisputed leader of the group. One or two boys in the group having better physique challenged the supremacy of Chandravarman but they also withdrew soon due to higher intelligence and deeper understanding of Chandravarman of royal affairs and strategy of war.

Having failed to admit Hemavati into his harem, the lustful king of Kalinjar went berserk. He heard a lot about the exquisite beauty of the newly married daughter-in-law of his finance minister. He asked his finance minister to send his newly wedded daughter-in-law to his palace. The finance minister didn't like it at all but the king kept on insisting. The chief of army advised him to send his daughter-in-law alongwith ladies of his house and in his impregnable protection. Finding no support and no alternative, the finance minister of Kalinjar complied with the direction of the king most unwillingly. The king neither insulted nor molested the newly married maid, yet this news spread around in different ways. General public didn't believe that the libidinous king didn't do anything with the young girl.

As a result, finance minister turned hostile against the king. He vowed to finish the king and his clan. He met the prime minister, the army chief and narrated the ugly incident. Both of them supported him because they were also harbouring grudge against the King. Prime minister said, "How can I run all the affairs of the state whereas the king himself is drunk and is closeted with women. After all some decisions have to be taken with the concurrence of the King. People have loyalty towards the seat of the king. They consider him as incarnation of God. Therefore at least, I should pronounce the decision in his presence so that subjects are fully sure that the decision has the approval or seal of the king. King is the king. People don't understood that he is the king because we have made him so. One day, I felt humiliated when he drove me out of his inner palace. I had gone there to seek his order on emergent vital issue. That day I felt that I was not the prime minister of the kingdom. Rather I was a lower being than his kept women."

The chief of the army also stated, "One day I had taken the king for inspection of the stable, the armour and the army barracks. He was so drunk that he fell down. Then he started firing me in front of my soldiers for no fault of mine. I felt so insulted that I wanted to resign but I didn't resign as I had no other job. Being the army chief, I cannot do the job of a soldier. I strongly feel that I shall leave Kalinjar even if I get a much lower job else-where. But a warrior has to get a job of warrior only. I can not do the writing job. That is my weakness. The finance minister said, "The treasury is almost empty. I have money only to sustain the army and the King's palace for next three months. When I told this fact to the King, he fired me and asked me to get lost. The public doesn't want to pay revenue unless they are doubly sure that the compulsion to pay is from the king himself. He is not even ordering that or issuing appeal to public to pay land revenue. I cannot ask him to go and attend few revenue collection camps. You, very well know that he insulted our family. Our service for generations has gone to dogs. I sometime feel that it is better to commit suicide than to continue in this job. If I commit suicide then he will drag my young daughter-in-law to his inner palace and will never allow her to go out. Thus, I am living for sake of living. I have been blackmailed by the king. I am a moving corpse."

Prime minister advised both his colleagues to keep it secret and maintain silence. We shall draw up a strategy to drive out this tyrannical king. A wiseman is one who takes revenge when he is in a position to defeat his enemy.

The trio had many confidential meetings to decide the strategy to dethrone the unjust and whimsical king. They took stock of the rising organization at Khajuraho under Chandravarman duly backed by the money power from Panna which could overthrow the king. They decided to keep neutral in the event of a revolt or attack and allow the king to face the music singularly on one pretext or the other. They decided to keep the autocrat king in dark about the developments at Khajuraho.

News of discontent from Kalinjar were trickling down to Khajuraho. Maniram was happy that people were angry on the tyrant, oppressive, sex-indulgent and whimsical king. He asked Chandravarman, "Chandra, this is the time when you should attack Kalinjar. One should strike when iron is hot. I have heard that even the prime minister, finance minister and army chief are against the king due to his nefarious activities and misbehaviour. You should perform Krishna type operation against the unjust king of Mathura, i.e. Kansa alongwith milk-boys of Vrinadavan. You should personally kill him in his throne in front of his courtiers. Then your supremacy will be established in the land of Jhajhauti. Chandravarman replied, "Grand father! I shall abide by you. Give me sometime to make proper preparations for the operation after chalking out a foolproof strategy alongwith my colleagues. I shall also have two brave brothers from Mahoba who are even more brave and daring than me and are ready to join our group."

Chandravarman sat in deep consultation with his colleagues and chalked out strategy with minutest details. All his associates in one voice supported Chandravarman and said, "We are Chandellas. We either rule or perish. This earth belongs to the brave and not to the cowards The brave enjoy the earth. The cowards serve them. We have to put an end to the arbitrary rule of the present king of Kalinjar and his dynasty. His agents are even trying to kidnap girls from Khajuraho, Ajaigarh and Mahoba apart from looting wealth and harassing poor farmers by exacting excessive land revenue. This season, they have even taken away the foodgrains from the farmland of the poor farmers. They are not even paying wages to the soldiers. I heard that even his army will support us either positively or passively by becoming the mute spectators during our operation of invasion. We can not afford to wait for long otherwise an outside king will attack and overthrow him. Then all of us will also be enslaved by an outsider. Any further delay will cost us this golden opportunity dearly. This type of kings have this ultimate fate. Chandravarman divided the responsibilities among his trusted lieutenants to mobilize not less than two hundred of young and similar minded boys. Everyone took his job in the right earnest. Chandravarman started taking his physical exercises and arms training daily under the supervision of his physical trainer and teacher. Two brothers from Mahoba also arrived and Chandravarman kept them in his farm house and trio started final phase of preparation for physical and even violent bout with the unpopular and infamous king. Chandravarman sent his spies to Kalinjar to collect intelligence and to cross verify details of their strategic plan and route chart on the final day of onslaught. He entrusted the work of planning and strategy to a group of three of his associates who had found and brought these two boys from Mahoba as their most prized collection in their armoury.

Now, all was set for final onslaught. A message was sent through Maniram to the prime minister that their positions would not be disturbed. The prime minister in turn, made the finance minister to acquiesce in the plan of Chandravarman. The Chief of army was also convinced by the prime minister. Accordingly, the army chief sent most of his forces for revenue collection drives far away from Kalinjar. However, the prime minister advised Maniram to caution Chandravarman to be prepared for emergency war against some of the loyal supporters and the flatterers of the king and advised him to keep at least fifty boys to guard in lanes approaching the palace and fifty boys to take care of the outflank of the king.

Chandravarman finally draw the strategy as per the feedback received from the prime minister of Kalinjar. Chandravarman alongwith his associates proceeded to Kalinjar to reach on the day of holding of court by the king. The king was totally unware of the developments. He was only busy in merry-making. His administration had become so weak that it had no inkling of such at plan of sudden assault. Even the general soldier of the army was thinking of revolt for non-payment of their salaries for the last three months. As a result they and their families were almost starving.

On the day fixed, Chandravarman alongwith his strong two hundred strong supporters marched towards Kalinjar fort where the king was holding 'durbar meeting'. The march by Chandravarman and his group alongwith arms and explosive went unnoticed by the public. The king's intelligence network was non-existent. Chandravarman reached Kalinjar as per plan early in the morning and divided his associates into there batches as per plan.

The three teams proceeded towards the main palace where the King under the drunken stage was holding the meeting. There were hardly thirty people around the king. Out of thirty people, king's sycophants were more in number who did not allow truth to reach the king. Chandravarman led the main striking contingent which would overpower the king and enslave him.

At the gate, Chandravarman was stopped but the gate keepers fearing their life, fled away. Only one gate keeper resisted who was overpowered by the supporter of Chandravarman and was tied to a pillar by a rope. The force led by Chandravarman in few minutes was in front of the king.

The King asked, "Why are you here? You have violated norms of this palace and the court. You are under arrest for indispline and disobedience of the King's order."

Chandravarman replied, "O King! Today, you have to reply. I have come to ask you few questions on behalf of public. Today, you are the accused person in the court of the people."

There was pindrop silence in the meeting hall. It was a very unusual scene. None came forward to the support of the king as everybody could see hundred young armed boys having scarf on their heads as if they had came to run over the king and the palace. Their eyes were red and were burning with rage. Chandravarman asked, "You return those two girls immediately, you got kidnapped from Khajuraho and have kept in your harem. You release all other girls and women under your captivity. You pay back all grains or cost of grains, your people had looted from the farmers of Khajuraho. You have been doing nothing in return for the welfare of the farmers and the public. Revenue of the regime has to be utilized for the welfare of the poor and the needy in the kingdom and not by you for personal luxury. You can only use upto ten percent of the revenue collected for upkeep of your palace and maintenance of your royal family. It is at present reversed. Ninety per cent of the wealth is being misutilised by you for your personal pleasure and lust which is not warranted by any norm. Therefore, you are accountable to the public for all your misdeeds. You leave the throne and appear before the court of public to be constituted by the prime minister to account for all your injustice, misdeeds and unsocial acts."

The king under intoxication, could not grasp what is being stated by Chandravarman. He was so far habituated to listening 'Yes, Sir', 'Yes, King', 'Yes Maharaj', 'Yes Jahanpanah,' 'Yes Foodgiver', 'Yes Protector'. He got bewildered and ordered the Senapati (the Chief of Army), "Arrest this boy. Whatever he is stating is an insult to this royal court."

The prime minister at this intervened and suggested, 'Sir, whatever is being told by Chandravarman is reasonable. I suggest that you release all the women under captivity and the problem can be solved without the bloodshed."

"What nonsense!" King said. He ordered the army chief to arrest Chandravarman but the Chief of Army said, "Sir, I don't have sufficient men to arrest hundred men who are before you. Please act upon the advice of the prime minister and sort out the problem."

The King refused to relent, "I am the king of Kalinjar. I shall not reverse my order!"

"So be it," replied Chandravarman. He ordered his men to isolate the king which thirty of them did smartly. Then, he challenged the King, "Come and show your strength to me alone. If you win, I shall go back. If I win, you will leave the throne to me." The King agreed. The bout started. The King was losing and at one stage while going down to Chandravarman, he took out the small knife from his waist and attacked Chandravarman. Chandravarman was ready for this eventuality. He took out a hand vice known as baghnakh and tore off the stomach of the King. The King died instantly bleeding on the floor of the royal court. The whole gathering started shouting, "Victory for Chandravarman! Long live Chandravarman!"

With this, the unjust rule of the King ended. Chandravarman released all the girls in captivity and sent them to their homes or to Khajuraho. The family of the king was sent to the place of their choice.

Chandravarman didn't disturb the earlier set-up and assured to all, "I have no grudge against anybody. We only wanted to remove the tyrannical and whimsical king so that the outsiders or foreigners may not capture our great land. I assure that all of you will live happily. We shall provide you a better administration under your popular prime minister and intelligent finance minister. Only the army chief will be one of my men. Don't mind. We shall not retrench any soldier. We shall pay them well including pending wages. Allow us some time to streamline the administration of this great kingdom". Everybody accepted Chandravarman as the new King of Kalinjar by shouting, "Jai ho! Jai ho! Jai Chandravarman! Jai Maniram!".

6

Conception of Temples

Assuming the throne of Kalinjar, Chandravarman declared, "I am holding this throne as the custodian of your faith reposed in me by all of you. I am grateful and shall ever remain accountable for your tacit support. The king is a source of justice and his regime is for the welfare of the people. As I am young, I hereby entrust the work of management of the kingdom to your beloved prime minister and honest finance minister. But I shall watch their activities constantly.

If there is any injustice to anyone from this throne, please don't hesitate to come to me. My door is always open for all from the farmer to the landlord and from the man in the street to the man in the durbar. All are equal before me. I alongwith my young army will ensure defence of this strong fort which has been invincible so far by the invaders. The Moon will be the real king of this Chandella dynasty. I seek blessings of the Moon to protect this kingdom from the evil designs of its enemies. I also invoke the blessings of the Moon for the welfare of all the men, women and children within Kalinjar empire. I shall try to win over Mahoba and Ajaigarh and handover these states to strong and capable associates who will protect them during times to come. The danger to Kalinjar will be always from that side. All invaders enter from Delhi-Agra route. Real defence is to protect one's territory from a far distance so that fight may be on the enemy's soil and not within one's kingdom as war always causes lot of devastation of man and material. I am a fighter and I shall always remain a fighter. I shall ensure that people pay due revenue to the servants of the Kalinjar empire. The revenue collectors however, shouldn't indulge in corruption and excessives. If I get complaint and the complaint is found true, that revenue functionary will be put into the dark well as prisoner. I never thought that the dead king had so much wealth specially in gems and jewellery. These diamonds and precious stones will be put to auction and proceeds will be spent for construction of temples at Khajuraho and for other public welfare activities. Panna will always help us to provide finance for the proposed construction of huge temples at Khajuraho. Khajuraho has been chosen as the place because it is geographically secluded and protected from all sides. Firstly, invaders will not know it and secondly, it wil not be easily accessible place. Of course, finally, it is my place and my mother & her father will supervise the construction. I therefore, call upon the architects, men of knowledge and religion or any one of Kalinjar and around to come forward and offer his suggestions to me how to build a memorable temple of Lord Vishnu which will go down in history of India as the best monument of all times. I seek blessing of the Moon to give me strength, resources and guidance to fulfil this pious mission of the new kingdom of Kalinjar."

The first meeting dispersed with appreciation of Chandravarman. People at large were surprised and happy at the new type of announcement/ declaration by the young king who didn't come from one of the royal lineages. It was really a peaceful revolution.

People from all walks of life attended the meet to give suggestions. It was decided that the temple would represent all sections of society and would not be divergent from the typical Indian style of architecture. The Brahmans and priests suggested that basic sanctity of the temple should be maintained. This was the group supported by Maniram himself.

The other group suggested that temples should represent the pulse of full life so that all people may enjoy their visit to

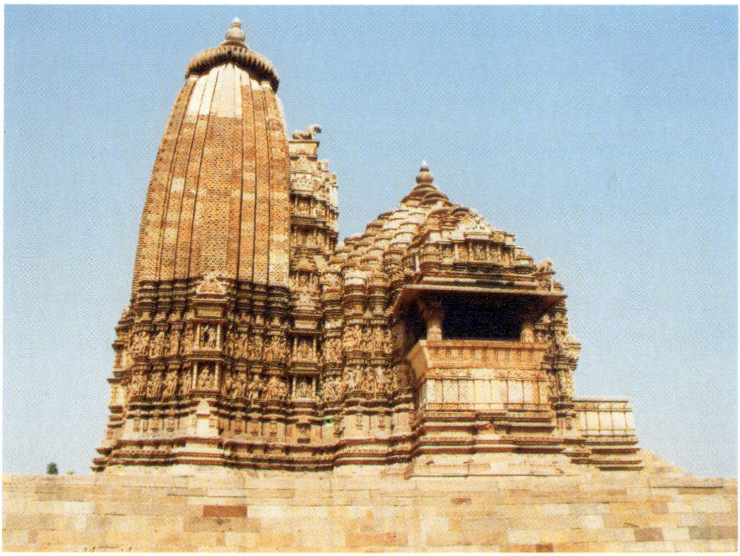

TEMPLE

the temple, starting from young folk to the old ones. In return, they should get back with a message from the temple.

The courtiers wanted that the temples should be generally the representatives of the wealth, victories and prosperity of the kingdom. Therefore, lot of wealth should be spent. It should be made very attractive for all from kingdom of Kalinjar and for the outsiders too. They should be impressed by the valaour and wealth of the Bundelkhand region.

A small section pleaded that the Hindu ethos should be represented in a new fashion so that persons leaving Hindu religion and embracing Buddhism should be attracted back to Hinduism.

The King listened carefully and gave general guidelines which satisfied everybody present. The temple would represent basically the vibrant human body. It was decided that the temple would be constructed primarily on the central Indian building style known as Nagara style of architecture mainly of sandstones from the quarries of Panna on the east bank of the Kenriver. The temple will be built strictly according to the Vastushastra. According to the Agni Purana, the temple is like a human body. The base of the temple are its foot (pada), the well is its thigh (jangha), and the spire is its head (mastaka on Shikhara). These would be adequately decorated by creepers, birds, apsaras (nymphs) mithunas (couples) and vyalas so that people might forget dark side of life and their visit might bring them good luck and pleasure. Decoration is auspicious. Accordingly, adornment (alankara) will be the important features of the Khajuraho temples and others temples in the kingdom. Chandravarman's mother Hemavati was happy that such a resolution was taken as one of the important policy decisions. It was further decided, "These will be lofty temples without any enclosure wall erected on a high platform terrace (jagati), which elevates the structure from its environs and provides an open promenade and ambulatory around the temple. All the compartments of the temples will be interconnected, internally as well as externally and will be in one axis, forming a compact unified structure. The essential components of the plan, viz.

ardh-mandapa, mondapa, antarala and garbha griha. The jagati-terrace will be emphatically high based storey consisting of series of ornamental mouldings which will slope out and grip the platform terrace firmly, providing at the same time, good light and shade. The wall portion of the temples will consist of solid walls alternating with voids of the inner compartments. The balconied windows, canopied by overhanging caves, will be studded with statuary of exquisite grace and charm so that people forget what they don't have in life or have lost in life. Above the central zone will be rising roof consisting of a series of graded peaks and veritably resemble a mountain range (Kailash or Meru). These peaks, arrayed along the axid lane, will rise and fall alternately, while maintaining their overall upward ascent, and will culminate in the tallest point or sikhara, which will be raised over the sanctums.

With these decision, the most important meeting ended with instruction to the finance minister to provide necessary finance and the prime minister to overall supervise each and every thing in details.

Everybody was happy that such a great feat was going to be accomplished during his Kalinjar regime.

There was a huge response. The initiative of the new king and the enthusiasm of builders caught the imagination of the entire population. Gifts in the form of money, clothes and jewellery, grains and other food grains, milch cows, timber, bullock carts, bamboo, ropes, iron ore, copper, borax etc. poured in from all sides. Stones, stone cutters hammers, chisels and sculptures were also sent by neighbouring kings, landlords, religious orders and associations. Even granite stone was arranged from long distances from Lalitpur and Rajasthan. A large camp soon sprang up on site at Khajuraho, humming with lot of activities. The sleepy place of Khajuraho suddenly awakened with work and work preached and exemplified by the Sungod. Everyone was happy that something historical was going to happen at Khajuraho under Kalinjar empire. The King ordered to be informed periodically about the progress of work.

The foundation laying ceremony was a great event. Lacs of people turned up for the function. The King himself got seated for the pious ceremony. The King appointed Rupakara as the chief architect. King Chandravarman ordered, "Oh Vasishtharasika & Rupakara! you have to fully supervise, control and ensure that at last two temples mainly Chausath Yogini and Lakshmana temple are built within next five years. The Chausath Yogini (sixty four meditating Buddhism ladies) is meant to attract back the Hindus from the Buddhism and also to prevent their further exodus to the Buddhism due to their Vajryana cult. Our Hindu religion is the eternal religion and it imbibes all traditions. In fact, the Buddhism is an offshoot of the old Hindu religion. The only thing, they have focussed more is free life away from strict observance of morals and discipline. We have lot in the old Hindu tradition. Focus on that. My reverend mother will guide you in this field. She is unnecessarily being blamed in the society.

The Lakshmana Temple has been chosen because I am a great devotee of bravery of Lakshmana, his restlessness for war and promptness to kill his enemies. I was told that in fact, Lakshmana is the same as Rama and they are same as Vishnu lying in heaven. However, the whole kingdom is the devotee of Lord Shiva. So you can have any number of temples devoted to Lord Shiva, the incarnation of Vishnu like Varaha (pig) or even Brahma though we do not have Brahma temple around. Our kingdom represents assimilation of all people, sects, castes, creed, cult, culture and civilization. We are against conversion of people by various sects by way of temptation, misrepresentation or misguidance. Let people have their free and fair choice of religion. People's will be free but their actions will be subject to law of the land. Give the full representation or reflection of our life style or culture and history so that visitors may not be required to go any where else to know about the real Indian culture and civilization and the Indian life."

The Chief Architect, the Head of craftsmen and Master sculptor bowed before the King and said, "We shall carry out the orders as ordained by his Excellency, the King of Kalinjar."

The foundation laying ceremony started with full religious fervour. A deep pit was dug in which seven metals and jewels were kept including iron, copper, diamond, pearl, gold, red jewel (panna) and dark brown diamond. It was a show of luxury of the Kalinjar kingdom which had undertaken such an ambitious project. Gold ornaments donated by the visitors also poured in. Midst the religious hymns, recitation of mantras, chanting of prayers and invoking of blessings of all gods, the ceremony was solemnized with great pomp and show. Enthusiasm and hopes were worth watching on the faces of subjects of Kalinjar who had only heard previously stories of king's indulgence into intoxication, hunting, killing or sex. The benevolent and public oriented activities by the state were hardly visible. Inspite of contributing profusely to the exchequer of the kingdom, the people didn't know any activity of the state for their welfare. They were left on their fate or on the vagaries of nature like flood, drought or storm.

It took no time for the king's treasury bulging more than Kalinjar itself. Temporary structures and tents were built for the workers. Thousands of labourers were deployed including hundreds of bullock-carts and mules. Stone quarries were worked out in the forest of Panna and Bijawar. In all, about one thousand people were deployed for the temple construction work on site. The finance minister met the prime minister and placed before him the budget position that the royal treasury would not be able to sustain that abnormal expenditure for more than six months. The prime minister sensing a failure briefed the king Chandravarman about the dire situation. Though the King showed a bold face before the prime minister, yet he started brooding over the matter. His mother Hemavati sensed the trouble and enquired about it from her valiant son. Chandravarman said, "Oh great Mother! I have started the project as per your wishes but it will be very difficult to carry on it beyond six months. There are no wars or victories followed by wealth at hand which will fill up the empty coffers. Please advise what I can do to save the royal honour and to keep up my promise to you."

Hemavati pondered over for a while and said, "Don't worry, my son. I shall find out some solution through your father."

Hemavati sent the message to the Moon through clouds, "Oh Cloud brother! After a long time, the hour has come for your test. You have poured down lot of your treasure on the land of Kalinjar. But look at my tears. Do something to stop these tears of your sister Hemavati. Take your beloved 'the lightning' with you and fly back to the Moon. Tell him that his beloved is in tears. His son is in trouble. He has started building the temple to save my honour and to communicate to people that our union was a natural phase and not that much immoral or illegal as people think. Sex is a normal urge of all beings and is the physical need. He is in deep financial crisis. I would not have troubled him. It is the last time that I am begging before him to save the honour of his royal son."

The Cloud heard patiently and flew towards the Moon. The Moon said, "Why do these mortals give me trouble now and then? I have kept up my promise."

The Cloud replied, "This the last demand from your beloved."

The Moon paused for a moment and said, "Wait, I am giving you a touchstone which could turn iron into gold."

The Cloud flew with lot of zeal and full of energy with the celestial gift and returned to Hemavati. Hemavati sprang with happiness and thanked her brother Cloud, "I am so grateful to you and my husband. God bless you so that you are never away from your beloved. All brothers and sisters on mother earth should be like you and I. You are instrumental to save my honour".

Hemavati went running to Chandravarman and handed over the touchstone to him. Chandravarman bowed down to his mother and expressed gratefulness by prostrating before her. Hemavati blessed the great son with all fruits of her good deeds.

After that, he became a confident king. The work on

temples was ordered to go in full swing. Lack of finances did not pose a stumbling block.

The degenerated tantric sects were great threat for the Hindus. They were anti-Vedic religion and rituals. The extreme tantric sects were kapilikas who were Brahmins' haters, the Kshepanakes (Jain) believed to stay without clothes, the Vajrayana Buddhists indulged in free sex and Charvakas were fully materialistic or consumerists. The people were fleeing and joining these Tantric sects because of flexibility and free life. Therefore, the Chandella rulers, started from Chandravarman adopted mixed Tantric-Puranic religion or culture. A ruler can not go all out against his subjects. He has to be their friend, philosopher and guide. The word Tantra means to 'weave'. Many things are interwoven on the Tantric path, including the lives of men and women. The Mahayan Buddha couples, later on known as Vajrayana Buddha of Tantric iconography celebrated this deep harmony of sense. The purpose of this dynamism was the creation of partnership devoted to the realization of the ultimate truth. For instance, the men cultivates pure vision by seeing the women as a deity, her sexual organ as the throne of enlightenment, and her sexual fluid as divine nectar. Thus, according to the Brhadoranyaka Upanishad, sexual union also constitutes a fine sacrifice, as performed by the creator god Prajapati Brahma upon creating woman.

> "Having created her, he worshipped her sexual organ.
> Therefore, a woman's sexuality should be worshipped.
> He stretched forth himself a stone for pressing nector.
> And impregnated her with that.
> Her lap is the sacrificial altar;
> Her hair, the sacrificial grass;
> Her skin the soma press;
> The depths of her sexual organ, the fire in the middle."

Vajrayan refers to the union of a lotus and Vajra, or diamond scepter. Uniting the lotus and the Vajra can mean uniting wisdom and compassion, or bliss and emptiness or bringing together the female and male organs to physical union, or a number of other things that must be combined on the path of enlightment. Thus, Vajra is male organ whereas lotus symbolizes the female sexual organ.

"The man (sees) the women as a goddess.
The woman (sees) the man as a god.
By joining the diamond scepter and lotus.
They should make offerings to each other.
There is no worship apart from this.
This is the dictate of Canda maharosana tantra."

Tantra asserts that, instead of suppressing, vision and ecstasy, they should be cultivated and used. Sensation and emotion are the most powerful human motivational forces. They should not be crushed, but harnessed to the ultimate goal. Properly channeled, they can provide an unparalleled source of energy, bringing benefits to society as well as continually increasing ecstasy for the undividual. Tantra deals in love, and love needs objects. One can not love nothing. Love means care, and care carried to the limit is perhaps the ultimate social virtue.

The temple architecture thus, combined the Tantric as well as the Hindu mythology to demonstrate bright and happy part of human life. The Chaushatha Yogini temple was no exception. In fact, sixty four were sixty four cycles provided in Vajrayana for achieving salvation.

The temple was built on a low rocky ridges. It was fully made of granite stone. It was an open air quadvanjuler structure, consisting of a courtyard measuring about 31m to 18.2 m and was enclosed by sixty seven peripheral chapels, each dedicated to a Yogini or an allied deity. The structure was extremely simple in plan and design, with hardly any carvings or ornaments, and had no architectural elegance.

The door-sill of the principal shrine was carved with three arrow-shaped flowers, the central one being larger. Its sanctum had plain walls and a plain flat ceiling carried on lintels resting on four pilasters. The pilasters showed a plain rectangular base and plain sheft of square section carrying brackets of a carved profile. The pedestals and the images however, were made of sand stone.

Some of the images of meditating ladies (yogini) carved out were of Himghalaje, Mahesvari, dancing Brahmani, Lakshmi eight-armed, Mahishasuramardini Vanquishing the buffalo demon is represented realistically. She has caught both the hindlegs of the buffalo with her upper left hand and has pierced his stomach with trisula (trident) held in one of her right hands. Her remaining three right hands carry fruit, broken end sword, the last held in the attitude of striking, while the remaining three hands carry shield, bow, and broken arrow. She wears dense head dress, ear rings, torque with pendant, garlands, necklaces, wristlets, undergarments fastened by a belt with jeweled loops and tassels. Her lion mount is shown on the proper right mauling the buffalo demon. A female attendant carrying lotus and kati attends the goddess on either side. A goddess seated in peaceful pose carrying fearlessness and pitcher is shown on each side of the halo.

Similarly, four-armed Mahesvari is seated in peaceful posture on a cushion and carrying trident, arrow, broken and mutilated staff.

Four-armed and three headed Brahmini is also represented with her great power and glory.

People were not attracted to the Chausatha Yogini temple inspite of holding occasional orgies. The purpose seemed to have failed. Then Hamavati ordered, "Build a temple with description of fullest life or wine of life. It should not be built in hurry. It is also not necessary that the art should always conform to the religious mandates. Art should follow the mandate of art only to make it eternal and universal. The art has its own way of representing life and the world. The art should first be successful. Then, we shall take care of its critiques. But we want people to come back to the Hinduism. Build Lakshmana Temple. Leave no stone unturned. It should be a better piece of architecture than the temple of Jaraimata at Barwa Sagar near Jhansi. We have been inspired by the

Jaraimata temple. But pupil should surpass his teacher. The future should be better than the present." Everyone got engrossed to comply with the orders of the king's mother. There was no other way except meeting punishment by death.

7

Construction of Lakshmana Temple

After the failure of the Chausatha Yogini temple, it was decided to have one temple which would be the flagship temple of the Chandella dynasty. The sculptors took it as a challenge upon themselves and pledged to satisfy everybody. It was then decided to construct Lakshmana temple because Chandravarman was brave like Lakshmana. The temple would consist of five broad categories of sculptures.

The first category would comprise of cult images. These represent calm and bliss and are accompanied by attendant gods and goddesses.

The second category of sculptures would have family life, besides numerous gods and goddesses. These would be figures in the niches or against the walls of the temple.

There will be guards with human figures bearing diamonds on the chest and garlands which constitute cognizances of gods at Khajuraho.

The third category would consist of the courtesans or heavenly damsels. These would account for the finest and most popular sculptures at Khajuraho everywhere on the pillars or ceiling, brackets or the recesses between pilasters in the interior. As per the Indian art tradition, these courtesans or heavenly ladies are invariably represented as beautiful and youthful nymphs, attired in the choicest gems and garments, and full of winsome grace and charm. As heavenly dancers, they are shown as dancing in various postures. As attendants of the higher divinities, they are represented with hands in offering or in some other postures or as carrying the lotus flower, mirror, water jar, regal dresses, ornaments etc., as offering for the deities. They are shown also expressing common human moods, emotions and activities such as disrobing, yawning, scratching the back, touching the breasts, reinsing water from the wet plaits of hair, removing thorn, fonding a baby, playing with pets like parrots and monkeys, writing a letter, playing a flute or sitar, painting designs on the wall or be decking themselves in various ways by painting the feet, applying collyrium etc.

The fourth category was to consist and consists of secular sculptures including domestic scenes, teacher and disciples, dancers and musicians and couples or groups. The erotic scenes have yielded some of the finest sculptured compositions in the world vibrating with rare sensitiveness, real life scenes and warmth of positive human emotions. The secular sculptures included scenes of army, battle, social life, different avocations etc.

The fifth category would consist of sculptures of animals and birds, foliage, bullocks, deers, boars including elephants, horses and vyalas. The architects had special facination for elephants and vyalas which they could represent in various types of background. The vyala is a heraldic and fabulous beast with different types of heads as situation demands, with an armed human rider on the back and a warrior counter-player attacking it from behind. Vyala has a deep symbolism as to how to overcome sex, desire or ego. One of such vyalas was christened as the symbol of the Chandella dynasty.

The work started in full swing. The stones were mostly mined at Panna and were shaped there only because already, Khajuraho was becoming a dump of stones. The cutting, chiselling and polishing of sand stones was very much time-consuming and labour intensive. Sometimes, the stones were broken in the process and all the labour was lost. It was also

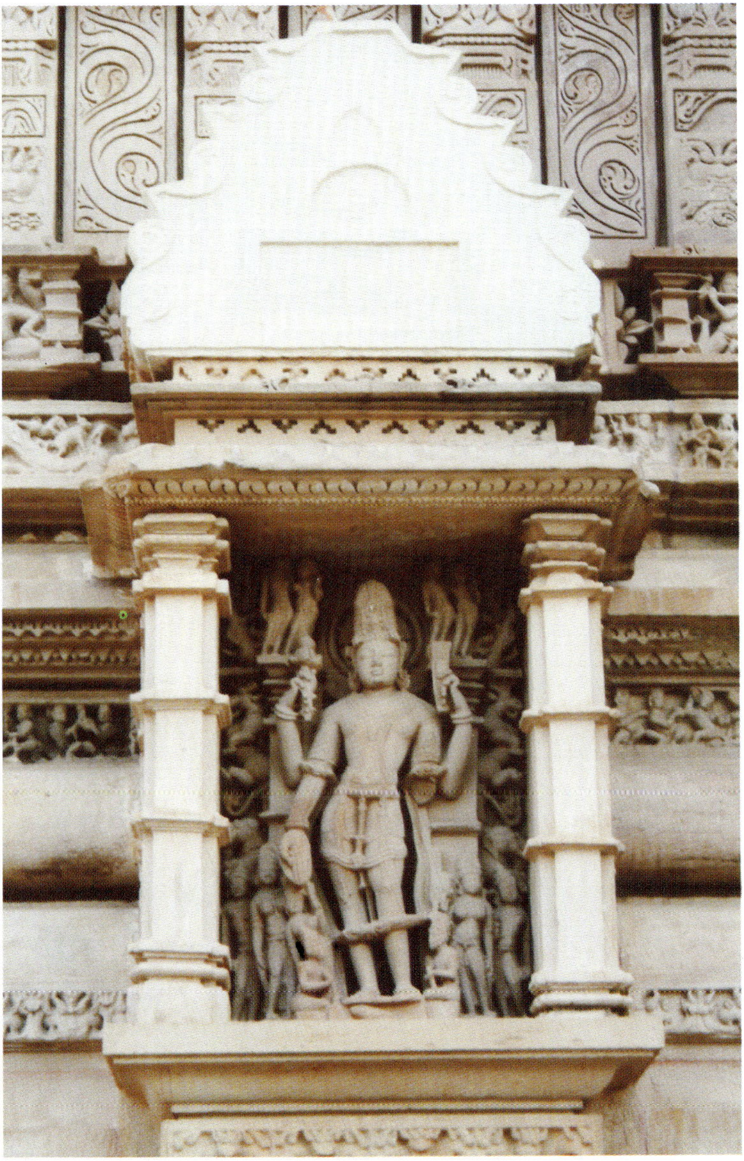

VAIKUNTHA VISHNU

difficult to arrange carriage of big pieces of stones by huge number of labourers.

However, it was easy to pay to labourers as the diamonds were also mined at Majhgawar from Kimbarlite pipes out of one thousand sq.km. area in and around Panna.

The platform (jagati) started after the ceremonial foundation laying by the king. Under the sanctum, the gold, metals, gems etc. were buried to make it auspicious. The ceremony was not so elaborate so that thieves and even foreign invaders might not be tempted to steal or attack and take away the hidden treasure. It was performed by the king in the presence of his ministers, family members, select priests and artists.

The platform was made ten feet high from the ground level so that no flood water could ever touch the highest point of the platform.

The platform has mixed of granite and sandstones. It had ornamental mouldings comprising of lotus scrolls, lotus petals, frills of triangles, pious decorated pitchers, hunting and battle scenes, processions of horses, elephants and soldiers, domestic and erotic scenes etc. The niches contain preachers, naked saints (nagas), gods and goddesses, ascetics dancers and musicians etc. The main temple alongwith four smaller temples, stand on the platform to be five great and pious agglomeration of temple making the edifice a 'panchayatana'.

The base of the main temple was raised with two series of mouldings. Then, the minutest mirror decoration work started. The walls were decorated by these small pieces of art like statues of lotus petals with a beaded band below, writing petals, grass petals, elephants in various poses including with the rider (mahaunts) procession of devotees, domestic and erotic scenes, figures of gods and goddesses.

All this work was causing drainage of royal treasury of Kalinjar. The king had received the touchstone but he didn't know how to use that. He approached mother Hemavati. She said, "Brother cloud was in hurry. I also forgot to ask him in excitement and jeal. He also forgot. Anything gifted by the divinity has strict ordeal to follow. The brother cloud will again turn after eight month during monsoon. Uptil that, you have to manage."

King Chandravarman had series of consultation with his associates followed by consultation with the formal royal army chief and the prime minister. It was unanimously decided to go for attack on Mahoba and Ajaigarh and capture those forts. As a result, lot of wealth would flow into the Kalinjar treasury which would take care of the great construction work.

Accordingly, Chandravarman organized his full army and planned to attack Mahoba keeping his two young and brave army commanders from Mahoba in front so that none could blame that he had evil designs to rule over Mahoba. He promised that he came for a better administration at Mohoba through the local chieftains only. The locals were convinced as two brave brothers from Mahoba led the attack of Chandravarman.

There was a fierce battle which Chandravarman and his associates had not anticipated. However, Chandravarman was constantly leading and ordering his soldiers in following war cry.

The Kalinjar people are great fighters.
They have shown their duties.
Whosoever came before them.
They defeated them.
Their clothes got soaked in blood.
The time period merged in blood.
The Mahoba's battle is fierce.
We have to show our best.

This appeal from the king mounted on the elephant changed the swing of the battle. The forces of Kalinjar fought so well that the king of Mahoba alongwith his army surrendered. Then Chandravarman arrested him and made the two brothers Chieftains from Mahoba as joint rulers of Mahoba. In the return, Chandravarman got lot of wealth.

Hearing about the fierce battle of Mahoba, the king of Ajaigarh surrendered to Chandravarman without fight and gave him lot of gifts in the form of gold, diamonds, gems and jewels on his return journey from Mahoba.

The aged king of Ajaigarh begged to migrate to Kashi which Chandravarman happily accepted.

Finding Khajuraho well protected from all sides, Chandravarman then put all his attention in completion of the Lakshmana temple. He in the process to collect fund for the construction of temple, got so much wealth which was sufficient to run his administration for a year apart from unhindered construction work for full one year. From these, the King brought ten elephants loaded with gems, jewels, gold and coins which were mostly deposited with the finance officer in charge of construction at Khajuraho.

Finding financial position of his kingdom adequate alongwith surplus deposit at Khajuraho, Chandravarman ordered to start the work on a simple temple where his grandfather had been worshipping at Khajuraho. He ordered, "The tallest Shivalinga in the country should be installed in this temple." He also ordered to start the Brahma (The creator) temple which was not so popular in the countryside. After lot of consultation, it was decided first to replicate the varah (boar) incarnation of Lord Vishnu along with best carvings on it. It was to be one of the heaviest idol of Lord Vishnu.

The Chief Architect and others got engaged to carry out the latest orders of the king. None had the courage to contradict the same before Chandravarman though Chandravarman always welcomed dissent. After the victory of Mahoba, he became the undisputed Chandella king of the area. However, he declined to erect a gate to celebrate his victory. Instead, he instructed his deputies at Mahoba to start some work on temple and tanks at Mahoba so that Mahoba could also flourish like Khajuraho. Water was a great problem in Mahoba. Therefore, digging of tanks was given first priority in the public interest. Chandravarman ordered that Chandellas believed to be the best in every field. The tanks at Mahoba should be the largest and deepest having eternal source of water.

After the victories of Mahoba and Ajaigarh, Chandravarman became the sovereign king of Bundelkhand whose kingdom spread from Kaimur-Vindhya range of mountains to Yamuna and Betwa rivers.

His instruction to build Lord Shiva's temple for Maniram was carried out within six months on priority. The temple had largest Shivalinga of the North India. The chief sculptor declared before the king, "It is not only the largest, it is the biggest in the Aryavarta. King rewarded the Chief Architect and his team suitably. Standing on a lobby platform terrace and tall base, it is approached by an imposing flight of steps. It has balconied windows in the cardinal projections on the three sides, while the frontal projection consists of on entrance porch. The pillars of this temple are stumpy and austere. They carry plain capitals and brackets. The stupendous size of the Shiva-linga occupies nearly the entire span of the interior leaving no space for ornamental works. As a result, Maniram was so thrilled that he started worshipping in the temple though some work was still going on. The temple was named by Maniram as Matangeshvara temple.

The reputation of Chandravarman spread far and wide. There were many women who wanted to become his queen. But Chandravarman didn't budge at all. He wanted to remain a full-fledged fighter king. Some people also developed jealousy towards Chandravarman, Hemavati and Maniram. They started talking loose about Hemavati and her affairs with the Moon and spread canards against the family. Hemavati however got information through the cloud how to use the touchstone.

After the adequate finances were arranged by Chandravarman, the crucial work on wall portion of Lakshmana temple started above the basement mouldings. Different groups of sculptors and workmen were hired for different types of panels. The strongest and most important three groups were made for modelling, moulding casting,

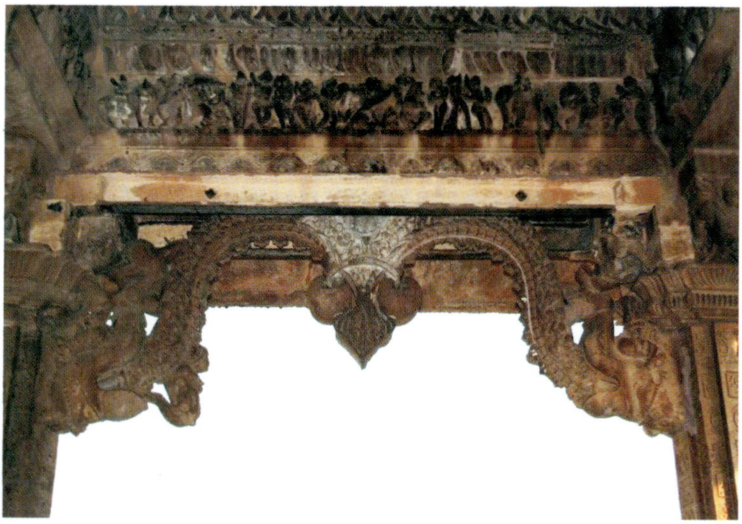

MAKAR TORNA

carving and installation of arched gateway, erotic figures and the main deity of Vishnu. The walls were decorated with two rows of sculptures containing figures of divinities interspersed with divine damsels on projections and sexual intercourse and erotic scenes in recesses. The divinities are always indulging in heaven in merry making. Therefore, erotic scenes among them in the mortal world can not be said very much out of place. The sculptures decorated in two rows stand on pedestals and are separated by a pair of band of stones reasonably decorated the lower carved with a frieze of attendants in reverence carrying garlands or playing on musical instruments. This row of panels is depicting scenes of dance and music.

On the facades of the main temple, there are friezes of army on march, hunting scenes, teacher imparting lesson in dance and music, scene of religious discourse, young woman playing with ball, disrobing, playing on musical instruments, holding on object against her enlarged breast alongwith killing of Putna by child Krishna by holding on to her poisonous breasts. There were supporting sculptures to the main panels consisting of nine stars (griha) namely Surya. Chandra, Mangal, Buddha, Brihaspati, Sukra, Sani, Rahu & Ketu known in English language as the Sun, the Moon, the Mars, the Mercury, the Jupiter, the Venus, the Saturn, and ever pestering two mythical monsters.

The main panels were gods & goddesses like Brahma, Lakshmi, Shiva and incarnations of Vishnu like Vamana, Varaha, Matsya, Parasuram, Narasimha, Kurma and supported by gatekeepers and god of wealth Kuber and his wife Rati. Without wealth, the construction was not possible. Similarly without blessings of God and auspicious look of nine stars, the construction work would not have been complete and successful. Then there was rise of the building in the ascending order like chariot showing support of large size flying bearded Garuda and two-armed divine couple. The front view of the crown has an image of four-armed standing Vishnu showing fearless palm carrying mace, broken discard, flanked by female attendants on either side. In recess, there are some mating couples. There are dancers, musicians in niches framed by pilasters. The naked saints are standing in reverence. The crowning ornaments comprise a large bell-member well decorated and the pitcher is embellished with drooping foliage.

After ascending an imposing flight of steps with two beautiful moonstone at the two lowest steps, one enters the interior of the temple through a highly ornate door hanging known as makar torna.

This is the most beautiful piece of sculpture. It is a work in stone as if the carving is made on the paper. The work is so minute and ornamental that one is wonder struck whether it is made of stones. It shows two loops, each emanating from the mouth of a flanking crocodile which has been forced open by a bearded gladiator carrying a sword in the right hand and a scarf like object in the left hand. A handsome male figure is seen seated on the proboscis of the crocodile carrying a lotus flower in the left hand. The loops are decorated with a running frieze of happy people or persons in copulation, carrying a garland or brandishing swords, or dancing or playing on musical instruments. The meeting point is decarded with a large pitcher pendant dropping from the mouth of figure conbining features of a lion, man, serpant and dragon. This is one of the most favourite decorative and architecture motifis of India.

The entrance pavilion to the main pavilion rests on eight pillars. Out of eight, four are interlinked. The ceiling consists of four concentric circles of coffered cusps with a long central pendant issuing from the centre. The interior of the main pavilion i.e. sanctum-sanctorum known as a garbha-griha forms one large rectangular hall provided with five transepts with balconied windows, two each on the North and South, and one on the West. The inner walls of this hall are quite plain in the lower half. Upper half has dancers, musicians, gods and goddess. Amorous couples are there in between. Perhaps, lower portions are kept plain so that people may concentrate only on the main deity but it is not understandable why mating couples are displayed even inside the sanctum sanctorum. It shows that the architects were determinded to show that the peak of desire i.e. Kama is the integral part of the Hindu religion.

Doorway to the sanctum is the Sun carrying lotus flowers in both hands, with the seven horses and a charioteer apart from all incarnations of Lord Vishnu, the main deity. The main rivers, the Ganga and the Yamuna are also shown as goddesses.

The main deity has three heads, of which the principal one is human and the side heads, can be recognized as that of a lion and a boar. The figure is four armed. All incarnations of Vishnu are carved out in stones.

The main deity is called 'Yogasana Vishnu' which means that Lord Vishnu is in union' with God. The main deity wears all types of gems and jewellery, torques, special immortal gem (Kaustubha mani), necklace, sacred thread, undergarments fastened by a jewelled belt with tassels and a double series of loops, ornaments on the four legs and ankles.

The Lakshmana has the most ornate sanctum with the finest finish and preservation. The quality of sandstone used for the sanctrum is the richest which imparts a metallic luster to the facade in addition to the enduring quality.

In the loops, there are mating divine dancers, loving birds, animals and humans in erotic postures including such abnormal themes as a bear or a horse mating with a human female.

Thus, Lakshmana temple is first and the last Temple of Kajuraho and can be called as the real representative temple of great Khajuraho architecture which has seen the world only with one eye unifying all creatures of the world though the attention of mortals is more attracted towards amorous and erotic postures.

Four supporting temples are proudly standing on the platform. They are small structures consisting of a sanctum. There are few sculpture showing gods and goddesses, guardian deities of the eight directions of space, i.e. Indra, Agni, Yama, Niriti, Varuna, Vayu, Kubera & Ishana, celestial maidens, dancers, musicians and other usual sculptures except erotic poses. It shows that Khajuraho architects had given more importance to sex and have made it a part of the theme of the main temple. Nandi, the bull of Lord Shiva (Destroyer) is placed with the main deity of Shiva. Its pinnacle is melon shaped member and is surmounted by pitcher etc. Even the approach stone is decorated by couch. There are images of four armed Vishnu (the Executive), the Brahma (the creator) and Ganesha (the first worshipped god).

The significant images on the facades of the Lakshmana temple include various erotic figures. In pedestal, there is an celestial maid holding her plaited hair in the right hand, and her left hand is placed between the breasts.

On the south face, there is an armours couple flanked by a nude male on the right and a nude female on the left showing that there was group sex in those days. In fact there was no taboo about the sex. But the architects of Khajuraho have abstained from depicting young girls indulging into sex or sex among the unequal in age or status. It means that the policy makers were conscious about the need for social equilibrium. They perhaps felt that healthy sex was essential for happiness in the family which springs from the sharing and satisfaction between men and women. Elderly people are incharge of households in the joint family system and they should be first happy themselves to ensure proper availability of wealth, goods and services for the requirement of other members of the family. It is questioned why the great sculptors only painted palatial women or women from the higher strata of the society. This is however, contradicted. According to one class of thinkers, the tribal women in the vicinity known as Kirit were equally well built and strong and were quite sexy. They used to indulge in free sex as shown in khajuraho as a part of their tradition. They used to put on scanty clothes and were almost nomadics. However decoration to their body can be the creation of artists to make sex a very joyous session so that people may forget all their dark side of life and enjoy orgy of sex from their eyes. At Khajuraho, even attendants are well crowned, decorated and ornamental.

Even in the inside pavilion, there is an erotic couple flanked by two nude persons one being a nude female attendant.

There are thousands of panels depicting the Indian mythological stories and symbols. The stories from Lord Krishna's childhood and youth have been vividly depicted. Each panel has been so carefully designed that it tells the whole story. This is the greatness of craftmanship of Khajuraho's sculptors. They seems to be more accurate and efficient than the painters with brush and colours working on paper.

Even then the king Chandravarman was not satisfied. He wanted that the work should go on and on even after his departure from this world. Mother Hemavati was in agreement with him and was grateful to have such an obedient son.

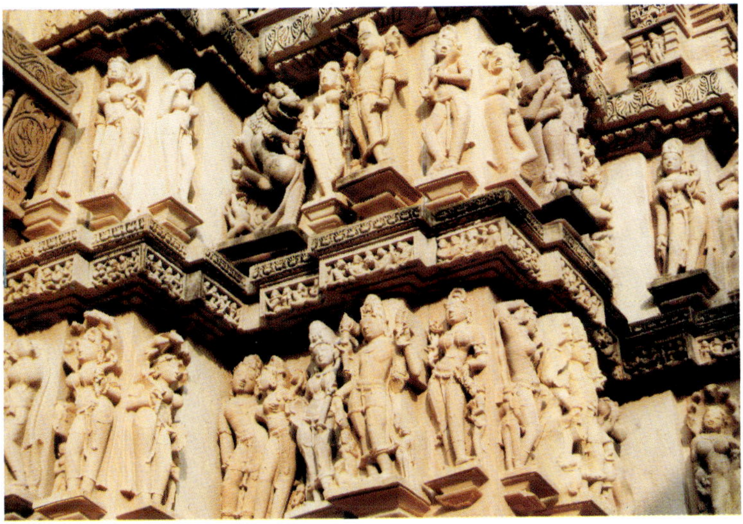

HAPPY LIFE

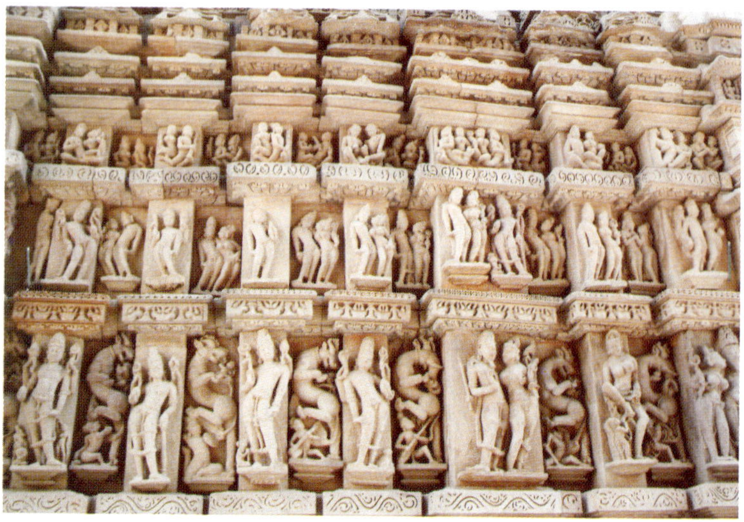

AMOROUS COUPLES

8

Temple vis-a-vis Erotic Figures

Few stone panel on eroticism had evoked lot of positive response from public. During preparation stage only, lot of people visited the construction site. It became a pilgrimage site. Many of the recent converts to Buddhism started coming back to the Hindu fold. They found that the Hinduism also had lot of free life and physical pleasure. They were unnecessarily attracted by the free sex indulged into by the Vajrayanites. They were unhappy the way, the Buddhist monks indulged into luxurious living cut off from the general public wherein the Hindu priests were still mixing up with general masses. They were living in Viharas known as monasteries of the Buddhists which imply halls, where monks met. These comprised of houses built having dwelling rooms and retiring rooms, store-rooms, service halls, halls with fire places in them, closets and cloisters and halls for exercise, wells and bath rooms and halls attached to the bath rooms and ponds and open-roofed sheds (mandaps). A devotee had built for his own use a residence, a sleeping room, a stable, a tower, an one peaked building, a shop, a factory, a fire-room, a kitchen, a privy, a place to walk in, a hot bath, a lotus pond and a pavilion. These buildings had valuable carpets, rug, pillows, curtains and such other luxurious decorations as were prevalent in high society of that period.

Buddha even allowed monks to care for their family or

take food or wear clothes. In course of time, the monks indulged in pleasures and lot of sex. Their lifestyle isolated them from common people. The Tantrik cult even went one step ahead of Vajryani Buddhists.

When the common people found that sex was not a taboo and was not prohibited in Hindu religion as was then advocated by the orthodox and moralistic Hindu priests like Maniram, they turned back to Hinduism. Erotic carvings at Khajuraho temples with royal patronage convinced them. Chandravarman was happy that he could fulfil the wishes of his mother Hemavati and could tackle one of the major problem of his regime i.e. mass exodus from the Hinduism to the Buddhism.

But his late found ideology didn't find support among the conservative Hindu theologians. According to them, free sex would disturb the equilibrium of the society. The division of society into four classes is meant that the matrimonial alliances will be amongst the same class. If it is violated, there will be problem of growth of the progeny.

The Indian society is a patriarchical society. In a free sex society, patrimony is not determined. Melathesis will result among crossbreed human beings. There will be lawlessness in the society. Observance of duties (dharma) and salvation (moksha) are more important than money (artha) and sensual pleasure (kama). Dharma and Artha are leading principles of the Indian Society. Physical pleasure should not be sought for, because it is an obstacle to the practice of Dharma and Artha, which are both superior to it and is also disapproved by meritorious persons. Pleasures also bring a man into distress and into contact with low persons who cause him to commit un- righteous deeds and produce impunity in him. They make him man not caring for the future and encourage carelessness and levity.

The opponents led by sage Vatysayayana says, "This objection cannot be sustained for pleasure being as necessary for existence and well-being of the body as food. Both are consequently equally required. They are, moreover, the result of Dharma and Artha. Pleasures are, therefore, to be followed with moderation and caution. No one refrains from cooking food, because there are beggars to ask for it, or from sowing seed because there are animals to destroy the corn when it is grown up. There is no distinction between 'sacred' and 'profane' love. All love is sacred, whether it is between a couple married according to the Vedic rites of going round the fire or with another woman, so long as the pull of desire to become one is between them. However, woman as wife should be honoured by the husband and the wife should maintain the chaste life for her, devoted to the man doing everything for her welfare. There is also strong need that the successful husband and wife should enjoy full pleasure in their sexual life. Therefore, pleasure in human life in no ways is less important than performance of duties or earning of money. In fact, the pleasure gives due impetus to achieve both these objects in life i.e. dharma and artha."

The votaries of 'pleasure' got majority. The prostitutes also joined their chorus. They stated, "We are not able to tackle large number of clients coming to us. It shows that they are not happy sexually in their family life. We try our best to teach our customers the best and practical art of sex but all is in vain. The male folk is so much in hurry that everything goes waste. There is need to impart sex-education to the man and woman and the youngsters so that after their good experience in bed during night, they could devote properly in their job or work during the day. Therefore, we want permanent depiction of art of sex. We therefore offer our monetary contribution to put erotic statues on temples."

The court-women freed from the vanquished king became very popular among public as they had professional experience of sex and pleasures during their stay in the palace and became expert in art of sex.

The conservative and the moralist group was not satisfied with the decision taken. They started picking holes in the story of Hemavati with the Moon-god and the way he begot Chandravarman. They found the priest Maniram as soft target who was devoting in the worship of Lord Shiva outside their farm enclosure in public at the newly built Matangeshvara temple. Maniram himself was a strict moralist intrinsically. He gave ears to the protagonists against erotic images being mounted on the walls of the temples specially on Lakshmana Temple being constructed in front of the Matangeshwara temple. He sent for king Chandravarman and within hours, Chandravarman was before his grand father as an accused person. Expessing his disgust, Maniram said, "Did I ask you to construct temples for depicting erotic figures? Templcs are abodes of gods and their sanctity is to be maintained at all costs. People have sacrified to safeguard their sanctity. Villages and villages have been evicted to protect the sacredness of the temple and chastity of woman. Many kingdoms have been destroyed and have been established for the sake of holiness of the God who is dearest to the hearts of all people. You are one who inspite of being the un-challanged king of this country, allowing such activities, which are against the tenets of the Hindu religion."

Chandravarman after longtime realized that there is somebody in his kingdom who could call him and fire. Bowing down his head, Chandravarman replied, "Respected Nanaji! I don't know the details of plan of work. I am the king and my duties is to ensure defence of the kingdom from all sides from all enemies. Secondly I ensure that the financial position of the kingdom is alright which can sustain our large army and can spare adequate funds for development of the areas under the regime and welfare of its depressed class of people. Beyond that I am not aware. I think that Mother Hemavati is in close touch with the Chief Architect and the Head Sculptor. Whatever she orders, is carried out. You have only taught me to obey the mother at all costs in all circumstances. She is the greatest of the great in this world for me. If you wish otherwise, I shall ask Chief Architect and the Prime Minister to see you, explain their position and take orders from you which will be subject to her concurrence."

Maniram was so happy with the response of Chandravarman that he stopped lending his ears to the protesters against the erotic sculpture of temples.

After sometime, he called the Chief Architect and explained his mind to him. The Chief Architect replied, "These temples are not simply places of worship. They are meant to be museum for the people so that the visitors can understand the whole Hindu mythology, philosophy, tradition and Indology. Temples are not only for Hindus but are being constructed for all subjects of Kalinjar kingdom under the universal king Chandravarman. Even Buddhists, Jains, Yavanas (Muslims) and Christians can visit these temples. Annual fairs, cultural programames and community festivals will be held in the premises of these temples. These will be centres of religious and social vibrations of people. They will infuse unity and loyalty towards the kingdom among the subjects. They will be platforms to protect our motherland from foreign invasion and slavery. Treasure will be hidden in these temples which could be utilized in cases of emergencies. These temples will in fact be community nerve centres."

Maniram said, "I don't want to listen to your lecture. Don't teach me what temple is. I have worshipped God all my life. I know what temple means. Can you show from the Hindu scriptures that such things can appear in the precinct of a temple?"

The Chief Architect replied, "All the Jataka myths and stories carry prevalence of youthful pleasure-loving couples. The poetry of free love of the fourth and fifth centuries A.D. like that of Kalidasa throws away the shackles of orthodoxy. Kalidasa has even described Shiva and Parvati in an erotic fashion. In the Kumara Sambhava, Kalidasa has depicted the triumph of the love god. Now-a-days, no thinking is left uninfluenced by Vatsyayana. Even Sankaracharya has described Kama (sex) in his Saundarya Lahari as;

"Kama has wanton made Thy
golden breast
Hard so that they might tear Thy
Bodice, and
Repose thy armspets. But he
could not harm

Thy waist; for it's safe bound by
Three cardamom lines"

Ultimate happiness lies in fulfilled sex. Sex is the ultimate ecstasy. None wants to talk of salvation (moksha) now-a-days. Even salvation can be achieved through perfect sex. People will be happy if they can get heavenly abode. Heaven is full of dance, music, damsels and pleasure loving. We can not teach a society which it doesn't want to learn. Reform can't be much ahead of societal chores. There will be no takers. They will treat you as your enemy and break away or distance from you gradually. A piece of art is one which represents full life. Without sex, life is incomplete. To implement your instruction, we shall have main deity in the Lakshamana Temple as 'Baikuntha Vishnu'. I tell you that none will like it. In art, greatest test of artist's capability lies in his ability to trace the naked sketches of man and woman in their utmost natural forms as these are fantastic figures made by God himself.

A woman's body is the best creation of God. That is the duty of every sculptor to represent. All coverings to their bodies like clothes, ornaments, flower decorations are made by man and therefore, these can be imperfect. The competition among artists or sculptors is how accurately, one can sketch the body of man and woman. If these are combined together, there can't be no bigger panorama than this one. I am in the field of art. I shall do whatever my dharma or duty in art ordains me. I can leave my job but I cannot leave my dharma (duty) as an artist."

Maniram was bewildered. He found that there were no taker of his concept of religion, morality, self control etc. He didn't want to disturb smooth going regime of his grandson Chandravarman. Let public get the art they like. The public has the reign they deserve. But he was not reconciled himself. He called the prime minister and affronted him. Expressing his anger, Maniram said, "What is this going on in the name of construction of temple? Are these all carvings of sensuality and sex? This is all opposed to our Hindu religion and culture. I hope that we are not destroying the Indian culture."

The wily prime minister keeping his cool with difficulty, replied with calmn and pose, "Sir, like you, I was also not in favour of erotic figures and carvings. But the majority decided that the erotic images should invariably form part of our construction work. Without that life can not be said to have been reflected in all its aspects. This was the common voice, the voice of the villagers and aboriginals who form the majority of this kingdom. You know that men and women wear scanty clothes in hilly and forest areas and they are the majority workforce in the temple. They insist that their life style should be directly or indirectly demonstrated in this great venture of the state. Kalinjar is a democratic state and that is its strength. As you know well that there is no sign of rebellion in this vast empire as the subject knows that her king is a benevolent and ascetic ruler. He himself is unmarried and doesn't spend a single penny from the treasury on his personal life. Our king is not despotic, arbitrary and whimsical like previous rulers who were surrounded by courtesans and whores. He is above all this like a lotus in water, yet he unambiguously desires that people's will should be respected in his reign. Howsoever poor or weak a class of people be, the voice of that class should find place in the overall administration of the kingdom. He himself doesn't interface with our work least in the work of the Chief Architect who is the most prominent craftman in the country at present. He often says that he hardly understands the niceties and implications of art and architecture but at the same time, he has ordered us to build temples which will be the best in the universe and will continue to be the best in times to come. Therefore, the Chief Architect has to pay more attention to the universal and perennial features of his work of sculpture. Our king has provided all resources of men and material for the purpose and has filled the exchequer for the future to fulfil your desire. He is busy in keeping borders of the Kingdom away from the evil eyes of the enemies and is always busy with his associates to further expand its territory. He himself doesn't understand the eroticism. He has assigned this work to the royal mother Hemavati. If you want a change in the well laid down policy, please instruct me either through the king or through the royal mother."

Maniram in disgust said, "It means that you people are not going to change. Have you built proper space in temples for holding religious conferences, kitchen and dining? Where will congregation of devotees gather and relax before lowering down before the main deity? The visitor's lobby is a must in a temple like in the Lakshmana Temple. I hear that the great sacrifice of his wife Urmilla for fourteen years while Lakshmana was in exile with Rama, has not been shown.

The life of Rama has also not been vividly inscribed. I know the way out. I shall tell Hemavati and Chandravarman and instruct them that Chandravarman should get married soon. Then Chandravarman will know life in all its aspects. At present, he knows only arms, warriors, carriages, elephants, horses, strategies to fight and win wars and resources needed for the war and the kingdom".

The prime minister listened to Maniram carefully and retreated after paying respect to him.

Maniram had long conference with Hemavati but they couldn't reach to a solution on erotic figures. However, they merged on the issue of early marriage of Chandravarman but they couldn't locate a suitable match for king Chandravarman.

They then decided to leave it on Chandravarman to decide. Hemavati said, "How can we insist upon our king-son to marry a girl who is not fit to become the queen? The girl just after marriage will take the place on the left side of Chandravarman as queen and will be respected by all. I do not find any girl around us. I also apprehend whether Chandravarman will be able to give her time from his busy schedule of royal administration. He devotes to every minute detail of the royal matter himself. He is a man of character, yet he has no objection to see that the erotic carving work goes on and on. As you are insisting, I shall take him into confidence and know his mind regarding marrying soon."

When Chandra was confronted with the proposal of marriage by Hemavati, he said, "Oh Great Mother! I don't want to marry because I don't feel any need. Many wars are fought on woman. I don't want to fight a war for the sake of a woman. I hear that the women interfere a lot in the regal affairs by exercising their influence through their husbands or paramours as king or persons in high positions just because of their charm and beauty. Secondly, I want to devote my full time to the kingdom and its people in my life. Another woman in my life may also divide my single pointed devotion to you. There is none for you in this world. Therefore, so far you are alive, I want to serve you with all sincerity and attention."

Hemavati stated, "Dear Chandra, No mother likes that his son shouldn't marry inspite of possibility of division of love of her son between her and her daughter-in-law. This is the duty cast upon everybody in this earth to procreate and leave his progeny to keep one's lineage continuing so that one could be memorized by subsequent generations. Love is infinite. If you marry, your love for me will increase rather than diminish. Men on earth like you should marry so that you could produce your lion descendants, who will look after the mother earth well. Otherwise, this earth will be burdened by incapable and handicapped people. In the long run, the mother earth may break down due to lot of burden and pollution." Chandravarman sharply reacted and said, "I have started hating the institution of marriage after it was denied to you. Due to no fault of yours, a social stigma was cast on you by this strange system of marriage and you had to suffer a lot for all these years. I want to enjoy life alone but I do not like that my subject should be like me. They should enjoy life in fullness. They should drink wine of life. They should marry, have children, enjoy sexual life from 25 years to 50 years of age and die happily. This cycle of life for them is unending. I don't know what joy they derive out of it. I find it a boring ritual. But if my people are happy, I am really happy to see them happy. I am not one who will impose my vahes of happiness on others. Opinion of Chandravarman was duly communicated to Maniram. The poor old man couldn't reconcile himself with his new wave of thinking. But he had no other alternative except to keep silence.

The so-called friends of Maniram will gather everyday around Maniram after he was free from his routine worship of Lord Shiva. They would talk from the grass of Khajuraho plains to the depth of Shivsagar tank, from the pebble on the street to the Vindhya peak and from the local maidens to the converted prostitute women now rehabilitated at Khajuraho. At the end, they discussed about various erotic figures being engraved on the walls of the temples. One would say, "Why are they showing lot of ornaments on nudes where a person during sex act throws away the ornaments and puts off his garments? Had these women possessed so many garments, they would have chosen the job of royal mistresses. These are all imaginary figures. Had life been so bright and charming, we would have left the shelter of God and would have adapted this materialistic way of life."

Maniram usually interrupted them and said, "Let us discuss something different today. A great public work is being undertaken by excavation of one mile long and one hundred yards wide tank under benevolent regime of my grandson. About five hundred workers are working on the job apart from workers working on construction of temple. The tank will be the life support system of Khajuraho. It will provide seepage water to the vegetation, plants and trees to keep alive. This is the greatest public welfare project, I can imagine. The monuments can not be sustained without green corner. Dry winds will cause corrosion on the hardest stone and will convert the stone into dust gradually. These dry and hot winds have swept away villages & villages in Rajasthan and ours is also a drought prone area. If there is a drought, such a vast storage of water can support the human and animals life at least for two years. People can not eat diamonds of Panna to survive. Sometime, even there are no purchasers of diamond in the acute drought. I have therefore, advised the king to dig the pond so deep so that the pond is connected with the perennial source of water which are many in the area beneath so many hillocks of Khajuraho. More than the monuments, the tank will be beneficial for the public. I have asked Chandravarman to name after my Lord Shiva. Perhaps it will be named Shivsagar. My Lord lives on Kailash mountain. I pray that he makes his abode in this tank so as to save teeming millions of this area from starvation and death. Whatever said and done, my grandson king tries to obey my instructions as far as possible keeping his duties as a king intact. But I am not sure whether he will obey my order to marry."

One friend of Maniram quipped, "There is no girl or woman suitable to marry with Chandravarman. Our king is a heavenly person. He is handsome like Moon, bright like the Sun and brave like Lord Shiva. None can be compared with him. We have to find some heavenly match for him."

Maniram replied, "We are old men. We cannot work so hard as to find out a match for Chandra. I shall again give him my last order to implement."

Everyday, Maniram used to gossip with his fellow people around temple. At home, Maniram's friends could not enter as entry was restricted by royal guards. These gossips used to whirl around and yet everybody used to forget about them the next day.

Shivsagar tank was excavated. People were very thrilled. The tank was inaugurated with the bath by king Chandravarman and offering prayer to the adjoining Shiva Linga at Matangeshvara temple under auspices of its chief priest Maniram. This was the greatest social welfare work done by the popular king. People started taking bath in the tank and then they headed for worship of Lord Shiva. During the Shivaratri day, there was great celebration. Thousands of people congregated. It was like the 'Kumbha bath' in the region. Everybody was happy and assured that the tank will not only serve the needs of local people of water for bathing and daily use, but also preserve the ecology surrounding the temples which will be the real protection of temples in the long run. During the month of Kartik (November), women of the nearby villages came on the banks of the Shivsagar in the early hours before sunrise to worship Krishna, the Lord of flute after bathing in the tank.

As Maniram was getting restive, Hemavati called the Chief Archiect and cross-questioned him. The Chief Architect was a learned man. He knew ethos of India well. He had learnt the Indian religious sanctums, philosophy and thinking of people by heart and had translated the same into his avocation or duty. He said, "Erotic sculptures have great significance and value. Kama or pursuit of pleasure is deemed to be one of the four purusharthas or duties of man and is regarded as an essential and indispensable preliminary stepping stone to moksha or deliverance, the final destination of life. The representation of erotic scenes therefore, are regarded not as abnormal or unnatural. According to the architectural texts, the depiction of the loving birds, animals and human couples is auspicious and brings good luck to the builder and vicariously to the devotees. Over the time, people also adapted to this belief. This constitutes a protection against the fall of lightning or the evil eye or ill-luck. There are many sexual motifs at Amravati Ajanta & Ellora caves and at Mathura in Lord Krishna's temple. According to our old Hindu view (sanatan dharma), the final aim of life is salvation which lies in the merging of the soul (atman) with the supreme being (paramatman) or the individual soul with the universe. The union of man and woman, wherein all sense of duality is lost, constitutes a symbol of liberation. As a man in the embrace of his beloved wife knows naught, either without or within, so one in the embrace of the knowing self knows naught, either without or within. The temple being a monument of manifestation, its structural symbolism leads from broad base to a point. Sex forming an important element of the broad base of life is, therefore, rightly depicted on the temple and such depiction is not at all in conflict with the higher spiritual purpose or the final aim of life. We have taken erotic postures from Kamasutra wherein yoga (spiritual exercise) and bhoga (physical pleasure) are alternate paths, leading to the same goal, the attainment of final deliverance. The great saint Vatsayayana has put the ethos of love between man and woman at the end of his work as follows :

> Desire, which springs from nature
> and which is increased by art,
> from which all danger is taken away by wisdom,
> becomes firm and secure.

However, at the end of the day, the chief has also to accommodate his subordinates' suggestions. After listening to the Chief Architect, Hemavati became speechless. She went into her memory lane how she became mad in the arms of the Moon as if she got deliverance & how she also couldn't afford to make lightning angry, the beloved of her cloud brother as she was already angry on her long separation from her lover Moon. Therefore in her own calculation, she agreed fully with the Chief Architect and became ardent supporter of his art inspite of strong opposition by her respected father Maniram.

Hearing rumours that erotic figures were being opposed by the very important person of the regime like the founder Maniram, some of the liberated and rehabilitated courtesans led by Poonam met royal mother Hemavati and vehemently protested, "We can not agree with the opinion being spread by the microscopic minority of Khajuraho that erotic sculptures should not be put on the temples. It will be the greatest blunder by the regime after the very successful bloodless coup by the present King himself to occupy the throne. Life is incomplete without sex. Sex is the major and the most important rather ultimate goal of life. We are getting so many visitors to us that we are not able to cope with. We are happy that our incomes are sky rocketing yet the same time, we are sad to learn that families are disintegrating. Our 'family' which is the basic unit of the society, is under serious strain of disstablization and collapse. Most of the sex hungry or sex seeker people accept that their wives are loyal to them but they complain that they either don't take interest in sex play or they become disinterested in sexual act after ten-fifteen years of married life and concentrate more on children or money or management of domestic affairs. After fifty years of age, no women is interested in sex. This is bad. As a result, our customers complain that their earning motivation and capacity go down considerably. They divert most of their hidden income to us. They are the people who form basis of income of the kingdom of Chandellars.

The life in the Buddhist abodes have added fuel to the fire. They want to emulate them. Therefore, to save families and Hinduism, we have come to contribute over hard earned wealth for this single purpose. I am sure that you being the number one lady of the reign, can best appreciate our support towards this genuine and social cause."

Without waiting for the approval from the royal mother, the group gave so much wealth to her that it could support all the erotic works on the temples.

Hemavati was astonished at this gesture. Her guilty consciousness evaporated that she was supporting the cause of sex-education or sexual life on the walls of the temples as she got lot of frustration and was having a void in her sex life except one and the golden opportunity for which she had been facing tremendous condemnation.

Maniram got the scent that the movement in favour of erotic sculptures had got so much momentum and people support that his lone voice would sound like crying in wilderness. But he himself and his moralist associates were not convinced and reconciled. They didn't lay their arms and continued to pinprick Maniram.

Maniram want into depression. He was lost in thoughts though the sweepers and other manual workers of his temple opposed his associates. They said, "Moral without food has no meaning." Maniram stopped talking to so many people. He even sometimes absented from the daily routine of worship. His diet was reduced considerably. He avoided public contact and everybody around him got worried as basically he was a good soul. His eyes lost the brightness and looked like searching something at a distance. He often became angry on the servants and maids who were serving him. He became a recluse.

Hemavati and Chandravarman were very much worried about the deteriorating condition of Maniram. Top Ayurvedic physicians of the kingdom were sent for but they found no treatment for shock to Maniram which remained undisclosed and couldn't be diagnosed by them. With the advice of the physicians and Hemavati, the King decided to marry himself soon with the hope that this would help to improve the condition of Maniram.

Luckily king Chandravarman had an inauguration of a large tank in hand in a village Rampura. He was welcomed and greeted there by the young girls and damsels of the village. Chandravarman fell in love with one of the damsels who had put the mark on his forehead and garlanded him. The love at first sight was so strong in Chandravarman that he took off his garland and put back on the breast of the damsel. The damsel blushed yet returned the love through eye to eye contact.

Everybody around was wonder struck and was spell-bound. Their King was always known to keep distance from the fair sex. A sudden change was pleasant to everybody. Public gazed matrimonial love in the eyes of their King for the first time. The small place was buzz with this unusual incident. King never responded to his reception specially by the fair sex during those days in the area. This was quite unusual and carried a different meaning as the King was bachelor and popular. Everybody wanted him to marry so that they might get good heirs of such a benevolent King to rule over them, protect them and look after their welfare. The lucky damsel also smiled and ran away. That was sufficient indication of her consent for his love. Who was the real damsel in and around Kalinjar who didn't want to marry Chandravarman? He was number one choice of all the unmarried girls in the region.

He was handsome, powerful and at the same time considerate, polite and popular. The damsel named Janaki, was grown up and bright. She had the sensuous fire in her which was making her the most attractive damsel around.

Though her colour was not so fair but her features were so sharp and attractive as if God had specially made her for Chandravarman. She was like the nymph, the architects were carving on stone at Khajuraho. Her face was shining with radiance, her breasts were bulging like the moon of the fifth day and her waist was thin like that of the lioness.

Chandravarman fell in love with Janaki and Janaki also blushed with love for Chandra.

After returning to Kalinjar, Chandravarman requested his mother to join for discussion. The prime minister came to know this unusual development even before Chandravarman returned to Kalinjar. The prime minister also ascertained from Chandravarman that he was interested in the girl, so much so that he would like to marry her soon. The prime minister sent a special and confidential messenger to Janaki's parents and they accepted the offer with pleasure. Their daughter was also in love with the young king Chandravarman and wanted to be his queen. Janaki's father said, "This can be the greatest privilege of any father in Kalinjar or around to give hand of his daughter in marriage with the great king like Chandravarman. We belong to the depressed class of the society and it will be a boost to our caste and all our ancestors that our daughter will be married in the highest family of the empire."

The messenger didn't wait for further reaction. That was sufficient for the time being for him to convey to the prime minister. He didn't commit himself as he knew well that the royal decisions specially in family matters keep on changing like fluid.

After the meeting with the mother Hemavati, Chandravarman decided to marry. Hemavati just put one rider before confirmation that she would ask reaction from her father. They both knew that Maniram would not approve the proposal. However, at that stage, both found that there was no going back. Maniram would reconcile himself with the passage of time.

Maniram was told about the proposed marriage of Chandravarman without disclosing her background. But

Maniram got some unconfirmed clues from his old friends. The marriage of Chandravarman with Janaki was solemnized with all grandeur. The mass of people participated in the celebration as the people's king married to a people's daughter in a simple wedding. Maniram couldn't go to Kalinjar to witness the marriage celebrations as he was too ill to walk. It was told in so many words to him by Hemavati that Chandravarman was marrying to fulfil his long cherished desire.

Maniram blessed the couple sitting in bed at Khajuraho. When everything settled down, the friends of Maniram came to know that Chandravarman's wife belonged to low cast. They then started poisoning the mind of Maniram vigorously as everything was being perpetuated against his wishes and against the great Hindu traditions and religion.

Maniram had lost power to withstand the mental and psychological agony with his feeble physical and mental condition. While talking during one of the afternoons, Maniram collapsed while gazing at the temple with his stony eyes and criticizing the erotic figures vigorously on the walls of the temples.

Last rites of Maniram were performed with state honour. He was honoured as the founder of the Chandella dynasty. His reservations regarding erotic sculptures and marriage of Chandravarman died with him without being made public as he was not in a position to distinguish between good and bad. It is the good for the kingdom which counts more than the individual good. His so called advisors or flatterers also disappeared just after the death of Maniram as they feared reprisal by the King and the public to have induced untimely death of Maniram.

9

Construction of Other Temples

During the homage giving ceremony of Maniram, it was decided that the construction of temples will go on. It will not be stopped just because the founder of the Chandella dynasty was not in favour of erotic figures. Kingdom is bigger than the dynasty. The people's voice will prevail upon the king's own ideology or values or his family's traditions. King is the representative of people's decision and he should reflect that in his speech and deeds whether willingly or unwillingly. After the marriage, Chandravarman had also become a vocal supporter of the depiction of sensuous aspect of life. Earlier he was keeping aloof from this controversy. Now he was enjoying new found love of his wife. His wife was strong votary that sex is the most important part of relationship between husband and wife. The king accepted the decision of the congregation happily. Addressing the gathering, Chandravarman said, "The temple by demonstrating erotic life of celestial maids or nymphs will take the visitor of the temple to the heaven where there is no worry, desire, jealousy, thirst, hunger, repentance or sorrow. There is only pleasure and happiness. Everybody likes to go to heaven. Why should only king go to heaven by construction of temple? Our subject should also see the bright side of heaven so that they perform good deeds in their lives and go to heaven. This way, we can also control our law and order and divert people towards development. Celestial damsels are the links between heaven and the mortal beings. Therefore, their depiction is a must. Women of our kingdom should also be like celestial women. Let us create all the prosperity, peace and happiness in our kingdom so that all women and men of this kingdom should become like heavenly residents. That is the ideal for the Chandellas. The Chandella dynasty believes in religious toleration. We respect all sects and religions equally but we can not allow some other sect or religion to misguide our innocent subject to its fold. We shall resist it with all our spiritual and religious might. We shall take back the misguided people to our Hindu religion fold which is ever shining and has proved to be relevant in all ages and in all places. I may not live long like my grand father but our great traditions will live long. I tried to fulfil all his wishes including marrying myself, yet I couldn't prevent his death. I seek his pardon on all of us behalf and regret his left over desire. Let God give him peace in heaven."

The meeting ended with the speech of the King. Inspite of being very democratic, the people feared Chandravarman and respected him by their hearts. As per tradition of those days, every meeting started with respect paying to the king and ended with thanks giving to the king after the address by the king.

Chandravarman called the Chief Architect and asked him, "Oh great Artist! I wish that you at least complete Lakshamana Temple during my lifetime so that I can die peacefully and can secure a seat in heaven. Secondly, I have no shortage of wealth for the on-going construction work. I don't know how my successors will manage such a huge expenditure. It is not always easy to defeat new kings and collect wealth from them. The Chief Architect replied, "The great King! You are the incarnation of God for people of Kalinjar. I have put all my family members and all the well-known sculptors of the area and surroundings on the job, but this job can not be speeded up beyond a limit. The real good artists are very few. We find that more number of panels are cancelled than are approved by us. We have to personally do the job. Formation of concepts take lot of time.

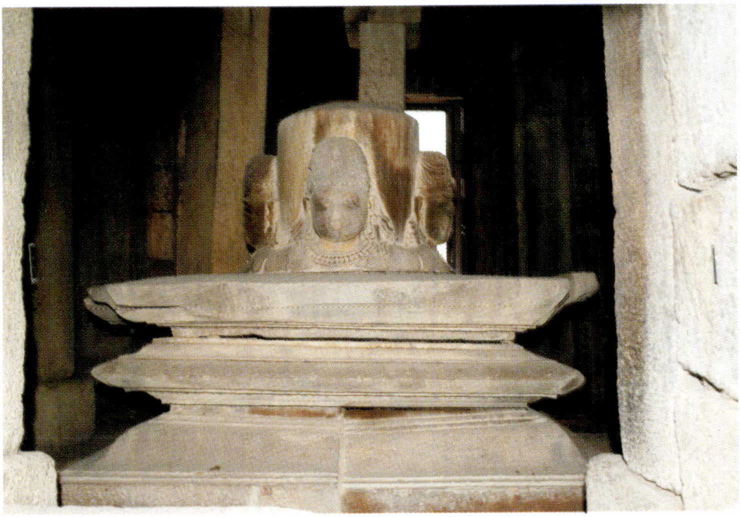

SHIVA

Learned persons and religious leaders have to be consulted before we start our work on a statue. We can not create a image or figure which may be rejected by the future generation. Therefore, allow us time. We are doing our best. Our families will continue to serve your successors. Don't worry. Even we die, the art will survive and will live long. We can not produce more than what we are doing. There is a limitation. Only one sculptor can work on one figure. If something goes wrong while working, the whole figure is to be rejected and all labour is wasted. One has to work slowly and steadily. We can't employ more number of artists as more artists are not available."

Chandravarman died but he couldn't see Lakshmana Temple completed. However, well before his death, he started the work on Viswanath Temple.

His son Vakpati continued the legacy of his great father Chandravarman. Vakpati was brave like gods and the great warrior like Arjuna. He extended the Chandel kingdom in South India like Rama had his suzerainty exercised upto the deep south in Sri Lanka. His son Rahul continued his great legacy and rebuilt the fort of Ajaigarh which was the bordering fortress to protect the great Khajuraho, the capital of sculpture in India. His son Harshdevvarman conquered the Rashtrakuta and reinstated Pratiharas in Kannauj. All the kings used the booty in victories for the construction of temples, so that future generations would remember them. Yashovarman extended the kingdom in Malwa, Bhelsa (now Vidisha), Mithila and Kashmir. Thus, he fully controlled the Bundelkhand region upto the river Yamuna. Yashovarman got the rare Bishnu Vaikuntha idol from Kashmir. The idol travelled on shoulders of workers, on mules and on bullocks. It travelled from mountains of Laddhakha-Leh through dense forests and valley. Then it came to Himachal and then onwards to the plains and forests of North & Central India before it was installed in Lakshman Temple. He had brought it from Kashmir after lot of toil and difficulties. Its journey was like a ballad written in nature.

His brave son Dhangadevvarman known as Dhanga ruled over for about fifty years upto his age of one hundred years and extended the kingdom upto Gwalior, Andhra, Kanchi, Kaushal and called himself Kalinjaradhipati. He repelled the invasion by foreign Muslim power in co-operation with the local chieftains most successfully. He completed the construction of Viswanath Temple and installed jewelled Shivalinga inside the temple. He encouraged construction of Parsvanath temple for the minority trading Jain community which shows his tolerance, large heartedness and magnanimity towards other sects or religions. By this time, the Buddhist sects of Vajrayayan and Tantric or mystical sects disappeared gradually due to their excessive inclination towards rituals and enjoyment. The Chandellas were the most powerful rulers of the Aryavarta except Indraprastha (Delhi). The slogan of his kingdom was;

> "The Indians are the great fighters,
> The whole world know them as such.
> They will not allow the honour of India to die,
> They do not know how to retrace back."

Finding his kingdom secured from all directions and treasury full of wealth, gold and jewels, Dhanga channelled all his energies towards construction of temples which were to be the great religious and cultural centres of the regime and were centres for holding musical conferences, staging dramas, delivering religious and moral discourses and celebration of Hindu and other local festivals and other religious gatherings.

The Viswanath Temple had all the facets of great monument. It combined thinking of his ancestors and of his age. After completion, the temple has ten armed dancing Ganesha on entrance pavilion in south with a serpent, twenty armed dancing Chamundaj, Lord Shiva-Parvati seated in peace, dancing Indrani with four armed & four armed Indra, dancing Maheswari with assurance, trident, spiral lotus stalk and water vessel, three headed and four armed Brahmani, dancing eight armed Virbhadra, four armed Agni, the god of fire, four armed Yama on buffalo mount, the god of death, four armed Krishna, four armed Varuna, god of water, four armed Vayu, god of air, four armed Brahma, the creator carrying book etc.

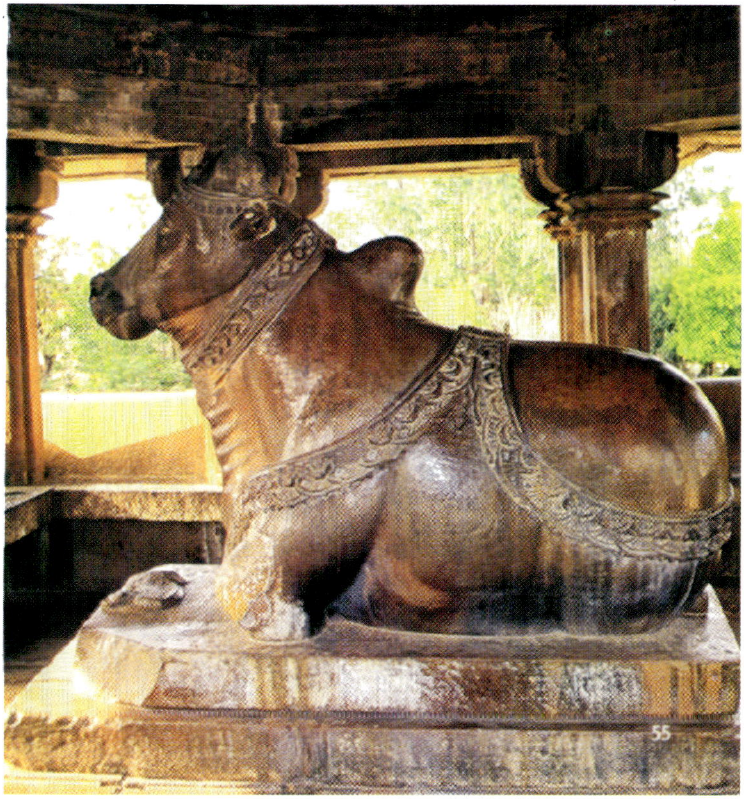

SHIVA'S BULL

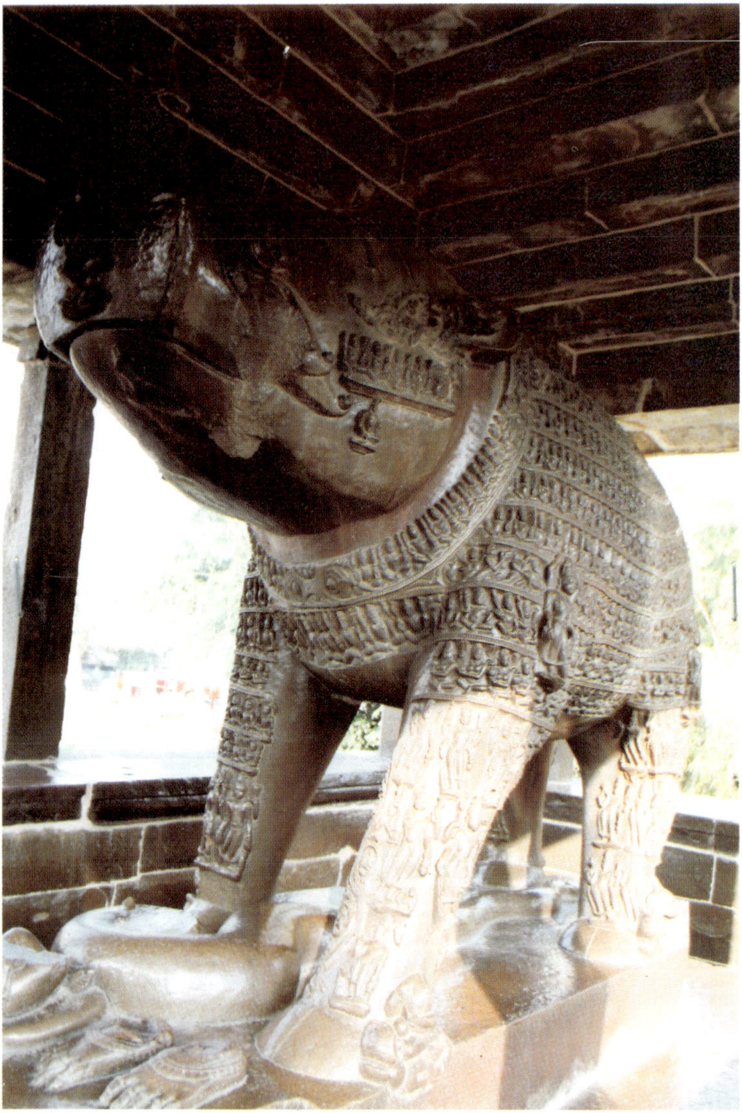

THE VRAHA

At all the places, images of Shiva are interspersed in hundred various forms. There is a group of two erotic couples. One of the females has covered her face with both her hands as she is feeling ashamed of exposing her sexual organs. There is another erotic couple flanked by two female attendants. The bearded male figure has both his hands placed on the shoulders of the female attendants. The main female figure covers the nudity of the right side female attendant with her left hand while she supports her weight upon her right hand placed on the ground. Four armed Kubera, the god of wealth is carrying spiral lotus, book and long purse.

On the sanctum, there is a twelve armed and three headed (the fourth one cancealed) Vishnu, the maintainer, four armed Saraswati, the goddess of knowledge, two armed Vasu, four armed and headless image of potbellied Bhairava.

A ten armed image of Nataraja Shiva with the head, legs and all but two right hands carrying skull cup and tabor broken off.

Inside the sanction, four headed Shivaling of good workmanship is installed. While three faces of Shiva are benign, one face is terrific as usual.

The temple Viswanatha amply demonstrates that Chandellas were great devotees of Lord Shiva. They intrinsically were Shevaits yet as kings they demonstrated equal obeisance to all gods and goddesses.

In front of the Viswanath temple, Shiva's giant size bull is made. It is 7'3" long and 6' tall idol of one piece of stone. Its temple has also twelve pillars and is decorated by necklaces and elephants in attendance.

After the victory of Kashmir, they brought the idea of boar Vishnu and the work on Varah temple started in full swing. They well knew that boar was very dear to Muslims and any work on boar will keep Muslims invaders away from Khajuraho. Secondly, Vishnu's incarnation as boar is one of the inseparable part of the Hindu religion and ethos.

The Varaha image alongwith its pedestal is carved out of

one piece of yellow sand stone and is exquisitely furnished to a gloosy luster. It is one tonnage stone measuring 2.66 m by 1.75 m having more than 675 miniature figures in twelve neatly carved rows. These figures depict all the important divinities of the Hindu pantheon, including Ganesha, the seven mothers, the seven sages, the eight guardians of space, the nine planetary divinities, the river goddesses, the seas, various forms of Shiva, and the different forms of Vishnu. In fact, the Varah represents the cosmic form, Vishwarupa embodying all beings. There is also an image of the Earth goddess.

There are about a dozen graffiti on the lower pedestal of the image and the interior walls of the temple engraved in that tradition. There are conches and flora decoration.

The Varah statue shows how efficiently the sculptors could work in different forms of arts. Even, one statue was made as full fledged temple depicting various images forms and figures on it. It was installed and consecrated in front of the Lakshmana temple, after their victory over the Pratiharas.

Another temple known as Parshvanatha Temple (950-970 A.D) was dedicated to the first Jain god known as Adinath during the reign of Dhangadev. The initiative was taken by Pahil, the minister of king Dhanga with the help of the small but rich Jain community of Kalinjar kingdom. The Jain community liberally donated for construction of their temple. Later the idol of Parshvanath was installed in the temple. The Chandellas had no ideological confrontation with the Jains and respected their way of life based on self-control and restraint. Their all gods are shown as naked depicting the value of self-control in life.

Therefore respecting Jain tradition of restraint and discipline, consummating erotic figures have not been shown on the exterior walls of the temple. But that does not mean that the Parshvanath temple is different from other temples. If shows pleasant aspect of life profusely.

The temple on the south east corner has four armed beared gods holding bow and arrows in usual celestial wear. There is also four armed Indra on the elephant mount.

On the exterior south face, there is god of fire 'Agni' on the sheep mount with flames coming out of the shoulder and head depicting fire very visibly. This is something unique imagination of artists of Khajuraho.

There is four armed goddesses standing with three bends, so also two armed god Shiva.

Three bends figures are very common on all temples in Khajuraho. It might be because of architectural reasons or due to mythological background.

One female is standing with three bends whereas celestial maiden is painting her right foot.

For the first time, story of Krishna and his elder brother Balaram has been depicted vividly on exterior of the temple.

The griffin known as vyala, the symbol of Khajuraho architecture has been for the first time depicted here with elephant face.

There are lot of figures of Lord Vishnu, his wife goddess of treasure Lakshmi and favourite Lord Shiva of Khajuraho alongwith females in various poses and actions. Special effort has been made to engrave goddess of wealth Lakshmi who is very dear to every one including the Jains. The Jains also worship her as goddess Padmavati.

The Lord of sex Kamadev is standing with his wife Rati on his proper right and holding embrace in his usual grandeur on crocodile mount with cylindrical headdress of three tiers, jewelled undergarment. Rati is equally decorated in her grace. Rati bore a look of Hemavati, the founder Mother of the Chandella kingdom.

There is a speciality of Parshvanath temple that it has many perforated windows which have been provided to keep cool inside the temple in the very hot summer of Khajuraho.

There are couples provided on all sides including divine couples but they are mostly in standing poses without indulging into sex.

There is god of wealth Kuber standing with his consort in his heavenly wear with mongoose shaped purse.

On south west corner, four armed Lord Vishnu has been shown in his moralist incarnation of Rama alongwith lot many divine couples.

North West corner, has nymph carrying mirror and other divine women. There is angry four armed god Parasuram with his consort Flames are depicted as anger coming out of his earring on the proper left which is the most appropriate symbol of anger.

In the interior, there are ten armed Jain goddess Chakresvari, Padmavati, Ambika, Manesi & others in calm poses. On the right is three headed goddess of knowledge, Sarasvati seated on a goose carrying book, water, vessel, etc.

Doorway of the sanction as usual is flanked by the gatekeepers known as dvarapala with their traditional arms.

Surprisingly around inner ambulatory, there are nymphs and erotic couples even one in action.

God of death Yama has been shown in ferocious face with whiskers and book.

God of water Varuna is with his crocodile mount. God of air is represented carrying flag with staff, book, fluttering scarf carried up like a canopy and water vessel. Deer mount is shown in the proper right. This shows easy mixing of the Jain and the Hindu cults.

As the financier Jain community believed more in wealth, Kubera, the god of wealth is repeated on the interior of the temple.

In the sanctum, originally, Rishabhanatha was placed on bull pedestal. Later on, black basalt image of Parshvanatha in nude was placed. There is no depiction of his meditation on five thousand feet high mountain peak in Madhuban forest.

The Parshvanath temple's figures of women show voheminous modelling like Lakshmana temple. There are tall celestial maidens with plump face and another one tilted head painting her foot with a colouring stick. The plump women have been shown equally active in love making. The leaders of the Jain community protested but turning down their suggestion, the chief Royal Architect replied, "We have a principle as a group. We take the guidance and expenses from the king or from you but we decide how to go about and what to make. We have certainly taken into account the basic tenets of the Jain sect of the Hindu religion. Your God i.e. tirthankars are naked. Then why should you take objection to the figures of women on the temple? It basically means that the person who comes to the temple should have self-control even in front of a naked or sexy or amorous women. In home or during night husband and wife are naked in front of each other. They should learn ultimately how to regulate sexual relation. That is the pinnacle of a man's achievement in spirituality. Secondly, through temples we want to provide places of worship to our common people where they can come and sit together, forget their failures, losses, sorrows, diseases and deprivations and are lost in heavenly pleasure for the time being to be able to go back to their families with fresh vigour and love and start working on their field or avocations with more dedication and diligence."

The financiers of the project of construction of Parshvanath temple were not convinced. They said, "At last, you don't make further erotic couples on the temple. The Chief Royal Architect didn't agree. They met the king Dhangadev and complained, "Unlike our religion and against over wishes and beyond our expectations, the Architects have made many nymphs in bending postures, carrying letter, holding a bunch of mango fruits, looking into a mirror, disrobing herself, painting the raised right foot, painting collyrium in her eyes, placing the legs across so as to emphasize the amplitude of the hips."

They further represented before the king, "Even in the inner ambulatory, the celestial maidens are mixing paint, removing thorn, helped by the barber, uniting a letter, supporting the right breast with the left hand, fondling a child held in one hand against her breast, yawning and clasping her hand placed at the back, disrobing while a scorpion representing sex creeps on her undergarment, even a headless pet monkeys shown crawling up on the thigh and disrobing her mistress, a woman looking into mirror, touching the breasts, painting designs on the walls, carrying sitar or guitar (vina), rinsing water from the wet plants of hairs, delicately touching her right breast with the left hand, carrying a letter while another hand is placed between the breasts in a thoughtful pose, plait of hair brought across shoulder to the front between the breasts, sporting with a ball in a dance pose, a baby touching her breasts, a pet monkey pulling down the undergarment of its mistress to reach a lotus bud held in her uplifted hand and a maiden meditating on the contents of the letter etc. We have no objection in showing a mother fondling and uplifting the child against her bosom and is stooping to caress it but they have shown an image of an erotic couple in action. The latter is very much against sanction of the Jainism." The King replied, "Dear protesters! We have on previous occasions advised the architects but they didn't like to be interfered with. Our founder great grand father had died due to this shock. I shall convey your sentiments but I can not assure how many of these will be fulfilled. If you want to withdraw, please withdraw and take back your whole money spent so far from the royal treasury. But you will miss the great opportunity in history. Such architects are not born on earth in every age. It seems that God Visvakarma has come down on the soil of Khajuraho and is himself guiding or heading the construction of these temples from the inception. None had seen such an art before nor anybody had heard about it. The vast majority of people is with the architects. However, as a king, my duty is also to take care of interests of minorities like you. I can assure you that I might be able to persuade the Chief Royal Architect at least not to create further erotic figures in consummating positions."

The Jain group was overwhelmed by the response of the King. They well knew that withdrawal from the project would be detrimental to their community. With folded hands, they said, "Sir, we are your subjects. We have come with a petition

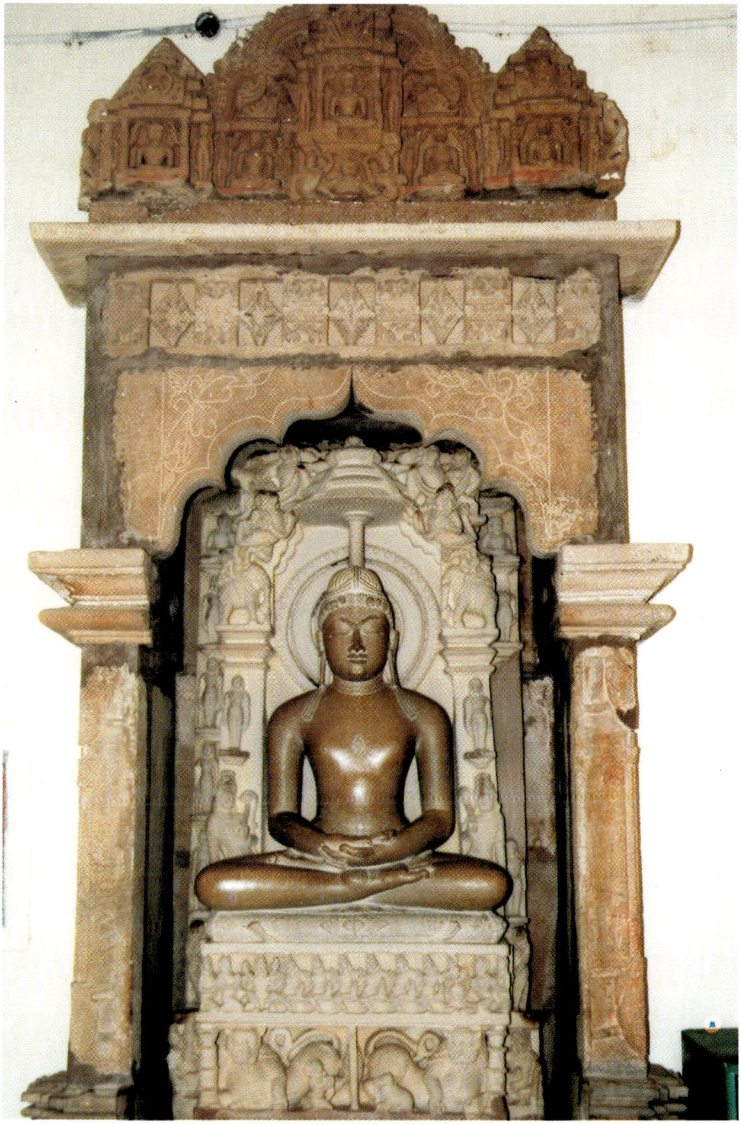

PARSHVANATHA

before your Lordship. It is you to finally decide the matter. We shall accept your decision as the final order or decree."

With these remarks, the Jain leader, took leave from the King and financed the remaining part of the Parshvanath temple and further kept an endowment so that the prayer on worship in the temple might continue in years to come alongwith necessary annual repair and maintenance of the temple and even the required periodical renovation as per demand of the edifice. They made a small group of the Jain thinkers who would interact with the Chief Architect and will have the Jain inscriptions engaved in the temples. It would have some reference of the person, who had contributed in making this huge temple and other Jain temples like Adinatha, Shantinatha and Ghantai Temple complexes. The style of writing should be simple and devoid of ornamentation. The language should be Sanskrit in 'devnagiri' in Hindi characters. Accordingly lot many inscriptions were engraved. The inscriptions would also carry some moral precepts through ethical couplets of the Jain sect which were results of thorough research and deliberations among the Jain saints of that time.

The Parshvanath temple which ultimately got completed, exhibits exceptional quality of the Indian architecture in stone which can not only rival any Jain architecture in India or abroad but can also be competitive with any Hindu architecture and will be rated after the Lakshmana Temple, Kandariya Mahadeva and Viswanatha Temples at Khajuraho.

10

Art of Kandariya Mahadeva Temple

The son of king Dhangadev could hardly complete the unfinished temples started during Dhangadeva rule of about one hundred years. His grand son Vidyadhara became the most powerful ruler of his time. He had the largest army. His kingdom extended from Vidisha to Gwalior and from Varanasi to Narmada. Thus, there was no problem to spare fund for the construction of temples. He started the construction of the loftiest temple at Khajuraho with a height of 101′ 9". It has the loftiest basement with the most numerous and elegantly ornamental mouldings which include two rows of processional friezes teeming with elephants and horses, warriors, hunters, acrobats, musicians, dancers, devotees and miscellaneous scenes of erotic couples. The sculptures of Khajuraho had exceptional expertise to make statues of elephants (like idols of Shiva everywhere). King Vidyadhara clearly instructed to his sculptors, "I shall take care of invasion by Mahmud of Ghazni. I shall mobilize all the Indian kings and defeat the plunderer. Before I die, I shall make Khajuraho protected from all sides so that the ill designs of enemies can not damage our great heritage. You only work peacefully and put your best skill in the job so that my temples will be remembered as the best temple in Khajuraho."

The sculptors designed a temple as beautiful as the Kandarpa, the god of love. Vidyadhara in fact kept his promise.

When the king of Kannauj, Rajyapal ran away from the battle field against Mahmud of Ghazani, he took charge and defeated Mahmud of Ghazni who had no other alternative but to retrace back. He also punished Rajyapal for that and killed him for showing cowardice against a foreign invader. Later on Mahmud of Ghazni attacked Kalinjar but tactfully Vidyadhara released three hundred mad elephants in the opposite camp of Ghazni and Ghazni had to enter into a peace-treaty with him.

Through his victories, he amassed unprecedented wealth and fulfilled the requirements of money and material of architects at Khajuraho to their satisfaction. Exploitation of labourers and craftsmen was foreign to the culture of the Chandellas.

As a return gesture to their King, the sculptors at Khajuraho put together all their knowledge, skill and attention to construct the best monuments to satisfy their King.

The temple had mature plan and design in symmetrical proportions. It was decorated with graded and ascending series of smaller replicas of itself, totalling to eighty four. For its maximum depth, it is known as Kandariya temple having cave like shape.

The Kandariya is the only temple of Khajuraho where the platform shows projections on the lateral sides and rear, corresponding to the projections of the transepts. The sculptures of this temple are conspicuously slender and taller and show the richest variety of celestial maidens (apsaras) in the most lively and often violently agitated postures. Exhibiting a mastery in the rendering of female contours and revealing a peak of conscious sophistication and exuberant grace, these sculptures represent the highest water mark of the characteristic art-diction of Khajuraho.

All the compartments of the temple including the sanctum have their own roofs, each higher than the other and each with a cluster of peaks around the central nucleus. The highest roof rises over the sanctum and culminates in the tallest pinnacle. Inspite of fatal fall of an architect from the apex point,

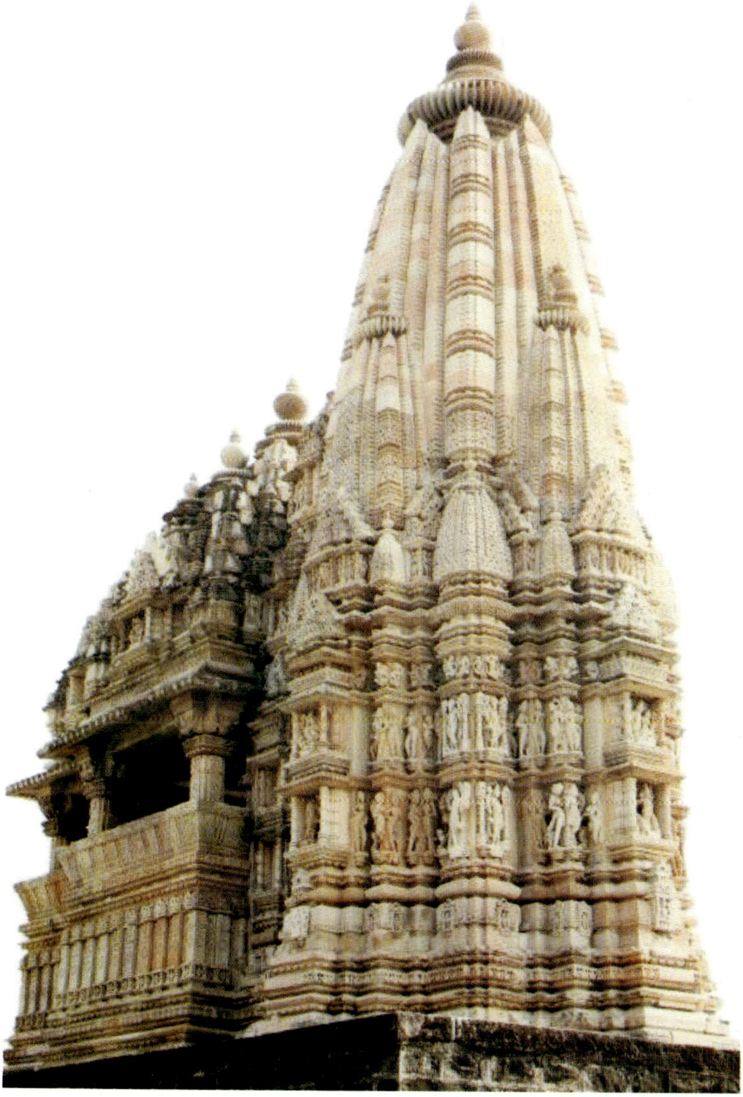

KANDARIYA MAHADEVA TEMPLE

the pinnacle of the temple is somewhat restless in movement though unified in theme and design. Perhaps no great edifice in India was complete without some sacrifice.

The temple is entered through an elegantly carved door hanging of four loops. The loops or garlands issuing out from the mouths are decorated with combined faces of lion, man, serpent and dragon, running frieze of dancers and musicians, some divine figures flying in air, Lord Shiva-Parvati, Lakshmi-Narayana and Brahma-Brahmani.

The sanctum is a square cell of 2.73 m. wide. A raised sandstone platform is supporting the marble Shiva linga in the middle of the sanctum.

On the outer side, there is one image of ten armed dancing Ganesha. A flutiest is on right and a drummer on left of the god. A seated four armed goddess occurs on each flank of halo.

On the southern side there is an image of twelve armed of dancing Chamunda destroying demons Chanda and Munda in ugly and ferocious posture with protruding eyes, gaping mouth, prominent veins and bones, dried up hanging breasts and a sunken belly showing a scorpion.

There are figures of four armed dancing Indrani, Varahi wives of god Indra and Lord Vishnu.

There is four armed dancing figure of goddess Vaishnavi on the western of the sanctum.

There are images of three headed and four armed goddess of knowledge Kaumari, four armed dancing image of goddess Maheshvari and three-headed and four-armed dancing Brahmani. They are all ornamental and are having attendants.

The temple is full of figures of Lord Shiva, the destroyer in different poses with variety of his postures decorated with serpents, ornaments and arms numbering about 131 accompanied at some places with his mount Nandi, wife Parvati, son Kartikeya and son Ganesha. Even Bhairav, the pot bellied enemy of Shiva has appeared thrice on his bull mount.

There are figures of other important gods like Agni, Kubera, Lord Vishnu, Brahma, Yama, Nirriti, Varuna, Vayu, Varuna, Vasu, Ishana which are repeated here and there.

The 'pediment' shows a four armed figure of Balarama seated in piece under a canopy of serpent hood. His body is well built and very elegant. He carries a wine cup. This is not confirmed by any mythological record. There is figure of four armed Gajalakshmi with standing female attendant and seated devotee.

Thus, the care like Kandariya is devoted to the cult of Lord Shiva i.e. Mahadeva in line with majority of the Hindu population of the Chandella kingdom.

The Kandaria also has volumes of erotic figures. From exterior to the interior, the temples has depiction of full art of eroticism just next to what Vatsyayana had described in his Kama Sutra, the 'Science of Love'. In the interior of the south face, there are three rows of erotic compositions.

The lower erotic panel depicts a sexual intercourse with the male standing upside down on head. It shows a nude female attendant on each side, while the principal damsel has placed her hands on the shoulders of the two female attendants. The male is pressing the vaginas of both the female attendants with his upraised hands. It surprises everybody, how with geometrical precision the males of those times could perform such acrobatics during sex.

In an upper erotic panel, the erotic couple is flanked by a nude female attendant on the right hiding her nudity with her right hand, and holding her scarf with her left hand. The couple is flanked on the left by a nude male attendant who is holding the left arm of the main female with his left hand. The man is bearded and is caressing the chin of the damsel with his right hand.

The middle erotic scene shows a draped female attendant standing, facing and on the other side a nude male attendant standing facing, holding his organ with his hand. The female attendant has placed her one hand on the arm of the man in

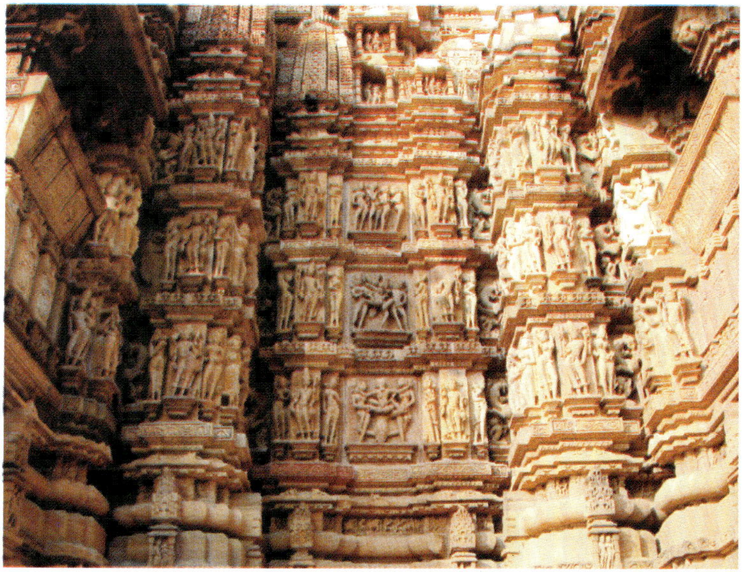

VARIOUS FACETS OF LIFE
IN KHAJURAHO ARCHITECTURE

action. The male attendant has placed his one hand on the head of the damsel. The heroin embraces the hero with her one hand and has caught hold of the hair of the male with her another hand. Thus, both are immersed into each other as single entity. The entire weight is supported on one leg of the hero. The attendants naturally wear an unconcerned look.

Many amorous couples are shown on the exterior very liberally. However, sex with animals has also appeared insignificantly on the lower pedestal. One panel also shows how venereal diseases of females can be cured in an indigenous way. The base of the temple has images showing oral sex, sex from the rear and copulating groups without any reservation. Like Vatsyayana, the Khajuraho sculptors made love holy by depicting at the holiest places of the Hindus. The figures reveal how tenderness in the approach of the two bodies, could take the two co-equals to the depth of each other and exalt the intensity of love in a style filling the physical union with a grace, that unified the human couples to the state of godhood. This is why in the Kandaria, the figures are definitely slender and have larger and thinner legs than those of the Lakshmana Temple. The female bust is also less heavy but more graceful. It is also the speciality of creation of the Khajuraho sculptors that mortal men are shown having sex with celestial maidens thus highlighting the importance of human life. In fact, celestial maidens like to have sex with mortal men. By witnessing the celestial damsels or courteous or royal females, one is lost in another world. This itself is the achievement of the Kandariya sculpture. It might be due to these erotic sculptures that the Khajuraho temples were spared by even the most barbaric foreign invaders or looters because they found these temples belonging to everybody in every age. The sculptors and artisans are shown in action with hammers and chisels. This is a true homage to the sculptors of Khajuraho. The hunters of aboriginal class or tribals are shown carrying hunted animals like boar and deer. Wrestlers, acrobats, gladiators, fighting elephants and lions are also shown.

Soldiers are shown in army procession together with elephant mount, horse riders, attendants, grass cutters, umbrella bearers, royal servants and attendants. The main weapons wielded are sword & shield, daggers and lances. Sword and shield are in many varieties.

The dancing girls and prostitutes are also depicted while dancing girls have been shown offering wine to their dupes, the prostitutes are shown naked. At Kandariya, sex has come down from heaven to the remote tribal village.

Many processions are shown with dance, music and gaiety.

Elephant running amuck and trampling men under the feet or tearing or tossing up the unwary with the trunk, are frequently depicted at Khajuraho. Fight between elephants appears to be a popular sport and is frequently figured at Khajuraho.

The celestial maidens are shown closing the eyes, playing on flute, touching the breasts, looking with the mirror, disrobing to ward off a scorpion, disrobing with the end of the undergarment, closing the eyes with one hand and hiding the nudity with the other, holding a bird. In one posture, she balances her simple body on the right leg and rhythmically turns round to remove a thorn from the upraised left foot as though in a dance pose. One is being demanded by her pet monkey whereas another is seen closing the eyes in a shy and coquettish manner. Generally, the nymphs at the Kandariya are seen with the back towards the visitor and the head in style of playing on a flute.

The love between man and woman is shown so that all danger of diversion from the wisdom is taken away and it becomes firm and secure in its objective. Even the sex act becomes the sacred means of salvation itself, the fusion of man and woman, where each becomes both, and together, they are freed of all bonds and merge with the cosmos. Appropriate couples have been shown otherwise any disharmony in physical body may create disharmony is sex act. Ultimately, both the living suffer. Thus, the object is to ensure joyful and harmonious living by husband and wife so that their sexual act may result into good procreation. Therefore, apart from adult and mature young woman, courtesans and celestial damsels immature young girls

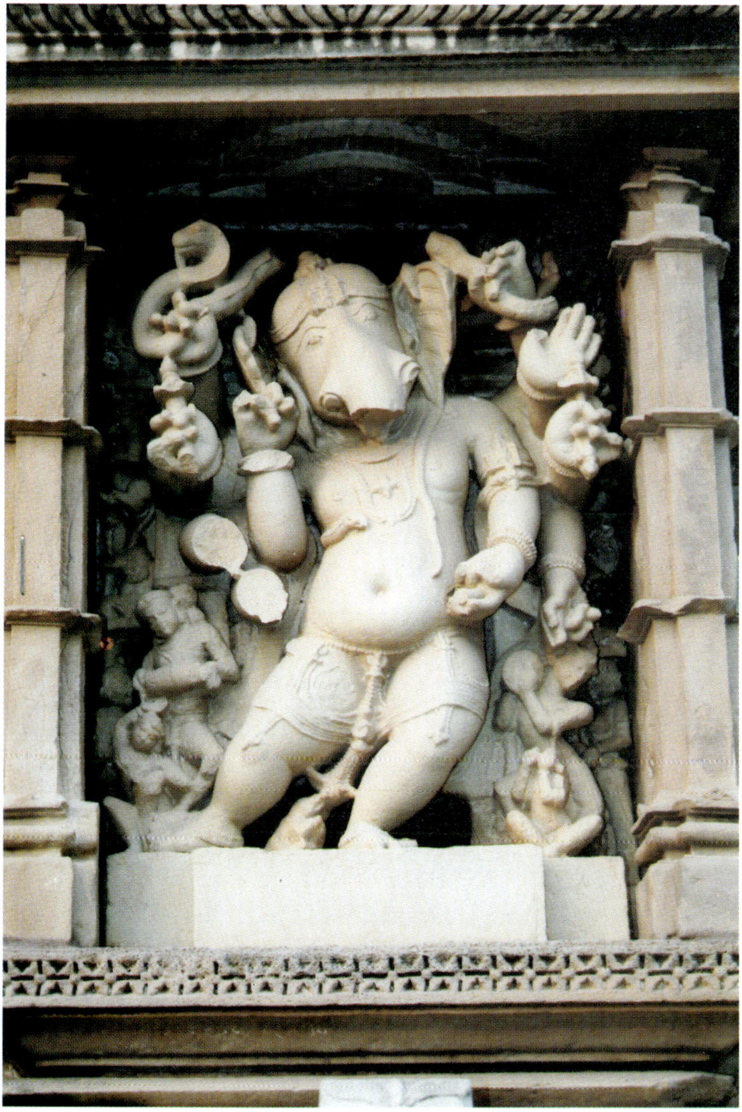

GANESHA

have not been shown indicating that they have miles to go before they indulge into sexual act as part of their routine or duty. Sex is as normal part of life as worship. After depicting most of important gods and goddesses appearing in Vedas and Puranas, the sculptors had no other option left except to venture upon creation of erotic figures. They have abstained from showing distorted sex or localized religious stories.

The great sculptors and artisans of Khajuraho have shown Lord Shiva in all imaginable forms. The choicest is the four footed Sadashiva image which is considered to be the 'unmanifest or manifest' aspect of the Supreme Shiva. His four feet refer to the four parts of the Shiva system that the builders of the temple followed. In the sanctum wall are depicted Shiva's manifestations as subduer of the blind or dark demon, the cosmic dancer and the destroyer. In fact Shivalinga is depicted as the "Primordial pillar of the universe". It is similar to the image of Prophet of Islam at Mecca.

Even the most religious devotee can not think of 131 forms of Lord Shiva which the sculptors have carved out in stone. Even the sandstone of the area has been purified. Lord Shiva wears the best types of ornaments, carries all types of weapons and is shown in his various moods. He is the God who is one with human beings, nature and the animal kingdom around. The bull around him feels so much at home as the cobra whereas his life partner Parvati feels one with all the people of Shiva. His great sons Ganesha and Kartikeya are the top gods in their rights. Therefore, it was but natural that the Chandella kings and the architects chose to make Khajuraho as the city of Lord Shiva though other gods like Lord Krishna and Lord Brahma are also there is their pristine glory.

A date was fixed for deification of the idol and to open the temple for general public. King Vidyadhara was the chief host. Scholars and priests came from Benaras. Lakhs of people gathered to participate in the celebration of the jewel temple of Khajuraho. The air was filled up with invocations of Lord Shiva by the masses. Lord Shiva is shown carrying trident, cobra and hand bestowing boon and another hand embracing

Parvati. Shiva is shown in many standing and dancing poses with lot of ornaments.

In many of the sitting postures, Shiva has a book. That shows special affection of the sculptors of Khajuraho towards books or knowledge. Knowledge is shown as gateway to pleasure. At places, Shiva holds a spiral lotus stalk or water vessel.

He wears earrings, crown, torque, garland the sacred thread, wristlets, undergarments, fastened by a belt with jewelled loops and tassels, and scarf and long chain reaching below the knees. The people had never seen their Lord in so many facets. However, hearing his applause and the obeisance of public to Shiva, King Vidyadhara addressed the visitors, on the pious day of consecration of the temple, "Today is the day of paying obeisance to Lord Shiva who is not only the Lord of our kingdom and people, but is also the Lord of the universe. Don't mix up me with him. He rules over Khajuraho. I am a simple devotee or attendant of Lord Shiva. You people spoil the King by proclaiming him the god and make him arbitrary. Let us plant so many trees in and around Khajuraho to make these structures invisible and inaccessible by outside armies so that enemies can not harm our treasure of architecture. I shall further request the Chief Sculptor to engrave the prayers for Lord Shiva so that Lord Shiva protects these monuments."

In compliance with the wishes of the King, a group of scholars and religious heads was constituted who wrote many verses in devotion of Shiva which were engraved in stones on the walls of the Kanderiya Temple. The verse became the main prayer for the Chandella kingdom.

> 'Om ! salutation to Shiva!
>
> May the dust particles of the feet of the Lord of the worlds be victorious by which even the bowing gods and demons are time and again brought to an unparalled high state of elevation.'

11

Epilogue

After the death of Vidyadharadevvarman, Vijayapala, Devaverman, Kirtivarman, Sallakshavarman, Jayavarman, Prithvivarman, Madanavarman ruled the Chandella dynasty in a gradual declining trend. During the reign of Paramardiveva, inspite of legendary bravery demonstrated by his two chief fighters Alha and Udal in war with Prithviraj Chauhan, the king of Delhi, the Chandella dynasty's moon eclipsed. The final seal of decline was put by Kutubuddin Aibak, the able commander of Mohammed Gauri, who reduced the Chandellas to the local ruler.

Afterwards, the heir like Trailokyavarman, Vivavarman, Bhojavarman and Hammiravarman fought wars to revive the great Chandella dynasty and won many parts of the lost territory but continuous stream of attacks from the foreign invaders like Allauddin Khilji and others kept on doing the damage and didn't allow the Chandellas to reorganize themselves and put a joint resistance to them. All Delhi rulers felt very much threatened by the stories of bravery and patriotism of Chandellas and they decided to take on Chandellas on their home turf at Kalinjar. Shershah Suri, the great came all the way to Kalinjar to subjugate Chandellas but died there while supervising his stable. Lastly, during the reign of Akbar, the Chandella dynasty came to an end in 1569 A.D. after two hundred years of memorable rule but the moon on the religious and cultural capital of Khajuraho kept on shining.

During wars with Chandellas, the invaders didn't bother much to destroy Khajuraho except few like Alauddin Khilji who is infamous for his religious intoleration. The kings of Kalinjar and Mahoba kept on contributing whatever means they had towards construction of new temples, completing the incomplete buildings and renovating and protecting the temples following high tradition of their forefathers i.e. earlier rulers. However, their contribution was not significant because the quantum of surplus wealth during those times was directly proportional to the territory one ruled.

Finally, at Khajuraho, Devi Jagadamba Temple, Chitragupta Temple, Vamana Temple, Brahma Temple, Javari Temple, Chaturbhuj Temple, Duladeo Temple, Khakera Merh, Vaidyanath Temple, Hanuman Temple and other medium and smaller size temples came into existence.

During the process of nature and history, many temples obliterated or were destroyed yet whatever temples survived, tell the story of the greatest Indian monumental legacy. Thus, the Chandellas have paid back the wealth to the nation many times more than what they had employed during their rule. In terms of pride and honour to the Nation, the pay-off is incalculable earned by these temples. Those rulers never imagined that in future foreign currency would be many more times than their gold and diamonds put in the temples by them.

The architects were careful about the impact of their erotic art. They therefore, did not expound unequal sex which are described by Vatsyayana of six kinds. One only sees three kinds of balanced sexual scenes i.e. hare with deer (female), bull male with mare female and horse male with elephant female in line with Vatsyayana's theory of sexual act.

The architects have also not vividly shown freeplay before coition. The kissing was not so popular in those days. They could have shown daylong activity of sexual union like in Konark, yet they have abstained themselves. They have not shown sexual union during various seasons. They have mostly shown amorous couples and in some cases group sex which might be prevalent in higher classes of the society

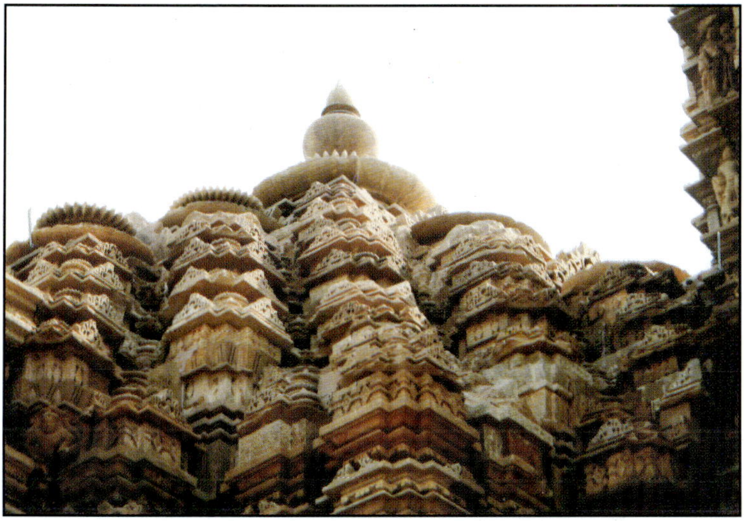

UPPER PORTION OF THE TEMPLE

during those times specially among courtesans. Similarly, they didn't patronize teenagers' sex which has become a problem of modern times. They wish that adult men and women in family life from the age of twenty five years to fifty years should have perfect union both mentally and physically so that they may work properly to earn adequately, run happy families, ensure procreation and collect enough riches to protect themselves from odd or awkward situations like old age. They strongly felt that the pleasure is a means to achieve aim in life including salvation.

It is a fact that the people indulge in cultivation and various other occupations. That was not the cup of tea of Khajuraho sculptors. That is also not necessary to the depicted. Art and literature depict something curious or important. However, religious and cultural facets have been demonstrated in all their dimensions. They had some natural bias towards their religion. The Khajuraho sculpture took care of all four aspects of life i.e. work, duty, desire or pleasure and deliverance. The Khajuraho sculpture is largely a secular sculpture. The artisans built like Titans and finished like jewellers on stone, while the musicians and erotic couples attract the eyes, willingly or unwillingly, yet there are many small engravings which reflect on the condition of the society at that time.

The sculptors have concentrated on happy side of life. They have created only few panels where Buddhists saints or Kapalika have been shown as laughing stocks by depicting either their unusual seized nude body or sexual action or their socially unacceptable rituals. It is a civil engineering marvel without much support of iron beams and only by way of pilastering stone into stone. These temples were used for the purpose of festivals and fairs as each temple has a hall of audience, dancing hall or festive hall and hall of offerings. These were the centres for social and cultural regeneration of the society. The temples were also used as platforms to fight enemies whether foreigners or internal. That is one reason why some of the temples were damaged and even destroyed by the invaders. The best forms of music, dance, drama and the moral formulations have emanated from these temples.

The Chandellas had perhaps taken inspiration from the temple of Jaraimata at Barwa Sagar in District Jhansi, U.P. when they were returning from war in the North. The last few successors had committed the greatest blunder because inspite of defeating Mahmud Ghazni on their turf, they didn't bother to organize other kings and didn't vanquish the foreign invader to the last and allowed him to flee back to his country. The Chandellas had the requisite bravery, skill, army and wealth with them but they did not have the broad view of nationalism beyond their extended territory. Secondly, in those times they neglected the very important strategical tact except Yashovarman that one has to fight his enemy on enemy's land. Otherwise, even if the enemy is defeated, its subjects will suffer lot of loss in material and properties. Thirdly, sometimes they fought on petty issues. As a result, the Chandellas were ultimately defeated and their territory was annexed by the great Mughal Emperor Akbar after about two hundred years.

The Chandella's age was full of prosperity. The literature in praise of young maidens flourished and was awarded by the king. While supervising the construction of temples, Hemavati died after few years of death of Chandravarman. But Hemavati's presence left indelible mark on the hearts and minds of sculptors of Khajuraho. People say that they depicted her in all form on walls of Khajuraho temples in gratitude. She kept on haunting the precincts of Khajuraho temple. Rumours go that she still appears sometime. All types of maidens including wine maidens, cobra maidens and celestial maidens have been shown in all possible forms on the walls of Khajuraho temples. These forms depict that woman is energy. There is sex in each cell of a woman. Man is consciousness. Sex lies in mind and not in physique. Therefore, proper union of physical energy and consciousness can do wonders in this world and can make this world a better place for living. As distortions, some lesbians have been shown and even magical monk is making love with a lady. At the same time, a noble man is shown giving advice or sermon to a lady to control her urge. These erotic figures also appeared to protect these magnificently and exquisitely carved temples from ill-omen. Similarly, worship of cobra has been reflected to protect the site from the earthquake. Thus, these temples provide an integrated view of the Indian culture. They also got lot of inscriptions engraved on temples by consent of the best scholars and leaders of that time which show the highest degree of knowledge of the Indian culture and ethos by the builders of the Khajuraho temples. The knowledge was picked up from the Vedas, Upanishads and other old scriptures. Locally, the stories of the Ramayan and the Mahabharat were very popular yet they went much deeper into original texts of the Hindu thoughts. Thus, the builders borrowed and adapted whatever best was available during that time in all fields. They more or less abstained from their local bias or prejudices. That is why these structures are ever lasting and universal in nature. Their achievement can be described in a sentence that the language of man has been defeated by the language of stone.

The various figures of gods and goddesses represent basic features of the Hindu culture. The temples contain only those gods and goddesses who are described in the Vedas and the Puranas and are closely related to our day to day life. Thus, the representations on stone are very practical and easy to understand. The common man visiting the temple can co-relate his life-pattern with the gods and goddesses appearing on the walls of the temple.

Lord Shiva not only represents the supreme state of perfection in man but in his very pose of Sadashiva indicates the way to reach it as well. The state of meditation shown in Shiva's posture is again symbolic. Meditation is the final gateway to self-realisation which is close to Godhood. The dancing pose of Shiva symbolizes the thrill of God realization. The third eye of Shiva means eye of wisdom so that one can pierce through the reality. It can destroy the universe. In the Hindu sculptures, ego is represented as a serpent. The ego serpent harasses one with its venom of desires. At places, desire for sex is represented as dangerous as cobra.

Man suffers all his lifetime from the presence of his own desires. Lord Shiva has controlled serpent i.e. ego. Shiva is shown in many places with a trident in hand. Thus three pronged weapon symbolizes the destruction of the ego with the proper combination of body, mind and intellect where intellect will be dominating. The laying down of the trident symbolizes man's victory over the three qualities (gunas) the satva (the pious), the rajas (the middle) and the tamas (the lowly). The lower hands of Shiva signify the offerings of protection and boons.

Shiva's tresses are long and matted symbolizing the continuous meditation and austerity undertaken by him. However, in the triumphant frezy, the tresses loosen and spread out which is the state of realization.

In the abode of Shiva, i.e. Khajuraho Shivalinga appears repeatedly as symbol of Shiva. Linga in Sanskrit means symbol. Shiva in this symbol refers to infinite reality. It is an ellipsoid. The ellipsoid is a combination of ellipses and circles. A circle has no beginning or end. Reality also has no beginning or end. The entire universe consisting of atoms right upto the solar system is in a way related to the ellipse. One half of Shiva Linga is embedded in the earth which represents unmanifest Reality, Shiva. The visible part above surface represents Shakti, the world of plurality which is controlled by Shiva too.

The sculptors of Khajuraho, have depicted ultimate reality in the universe by installing the idol of Vaikuntha Vishnu. The mortal beings can think of only the best pleasure world i.e; the heaven. Inspite of showing all heavenly pleasures, the thinkers of Khajuraho did not want to compromise with the ultimate realization which is Vaikuntha, the abode of Lord Vishnu which is the presiding deity of the Lakshmana Temple. Vishnu represents the power of sustenance. Vishnu is wedded to Lakshmi, the goddess of wealth. In order to maintain anything, the maintainer must necessarily possess wealth. In his four hands, Vishnu holds a conch, discus, mace and lotus. The conch is blown by the Lord calling the people of the world to lead pure and noble life. The discus is to warn the wicked or enemies to keep away. The mace in the third hand is meant as warning to draw man's attention to this stern law of nature that he will meet his disaster if he doesn't pay heed to the warnings of nature. The lotus indicates the final goal of human evolution or the supreme reality. The crown on Vishnu's head signifies his supreme sovereignty and lordship over the world. Lakshmi sits on his feet. Thus, wealth and prosperity will follow automatically if one follows Vishnu. Similarly, four faces of Brahma represents the four Vedas and the inner personality combining mind, intellect, ego and consciousness. The Lord in his four hands has water pot, sacred squared book, sacrificial implement and rosary. The animal hide worn by Brahma stands for austerity. He is seated on swan which has the ability to draw the milk alone and leave the water behind out of the mixture. A man should have analytical ability to grasp the good and reject the bad.

Goddess Saraswati is holding the book which shows the path of knowledge. Saraswati playing on the lute (vina) indicates maintenance of single pointed devotion to Lord through music and recitation. Similarly, goddess Kali or Durga represents the power of destruction. By invoking Kali the devotee is said to draw her mighty power to keep his all enemies at bay including all his negative tendencies.

Thus, there are innumerable meanings and symbolism reflected in the great art of Khajuraho. There are different hidden meanings of world and the body for the great scholars and architects of Khajuraho. For them, the space is the only garment for the man and woman. Even they have shown Shiva and Parvati in a happy mood to bless the people. One of the inscriptions announces, "May the laughter of 'Sambhu' while thus jesting with his beloved (Uma) be for your welfare".

However, the architects of Khajuraho have abstained from showing Shiva and Parvati as normal husband and wife whereas many scriptures and literacy works have even described Shiva & Parvati as worldly human beings. The architects or sculptors have avoided that and have confined themselves by depicting either ordinary men and women or royal courtesans or celestial maidens or nymphs in arousing sensuality.

The Chandellas were personally pious and moralist. They believed in piety. They observed one wife norm even being kings. At the sametime, they were generous towards their subjects and allowed the temple architecture to blossom in the courtyard of the common man of the area. Though by putting up erotic figure, they incurred the wrath of the founder of the kingdom, Maniram, yet they didn't deviate because pure art and sculpture required so. In fact, they communicated through stones that sex energy (kama) is very important to shape life and if properly channelized, can do wonders to make man and world happy and prosperous. They didn't impose their value-system on their subjects. Rather, they adapted the value system of their land, the Budelkhand. None could rival their personal valour at that time, yet they did not become despotic ruler or dictator. They captured other territories and the proceeds of the victories were utilized for the construction of temples. Some say that Chandravarman, the great built 85 architectural masterpiece temples and performed 'bandhya yagna' to wash away sins of his mother Hemavati.

The cuckoo still sings in praise of Hemavati on the trees when spring returns and the sky changes colours and exibits the infinity of nature's beauty every evening over Khajuraho. Some say that they did this to have fame on earth and to secure a place in heaven. But the fact is that they paid back whatever they had taken from the kingdom. The temples' sculpture reveals the pristine elegance of the ancient ideas embedded in the temples. They have given a heritage to the world which will remain immortal. This is the lesson that one can learn from the Chandellas to evolve himself to make this world a better place to live.

May there be happiness.

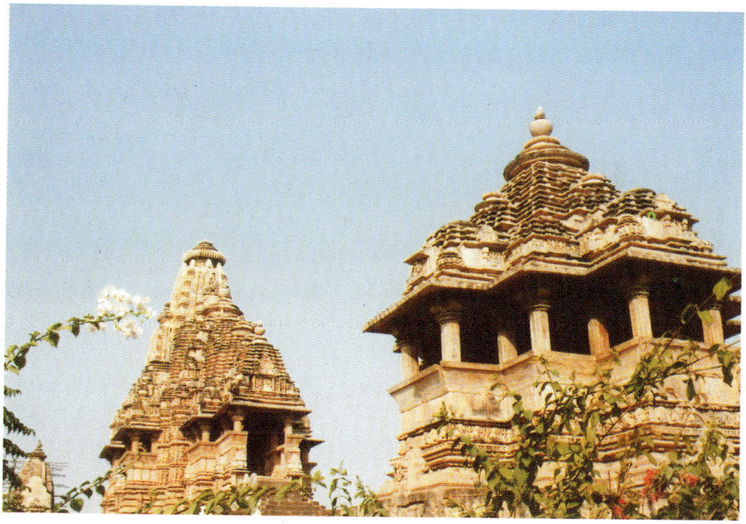

TEMPLE VIEW

Acknowledgements

Anand, Mulk Raj & Lance Dane (ed.)	:	Kama Sutra of Vatsyayana, Published by Arnold Publishers (India) Pvt. Ltd., AB/9 Safdarjung Enclave, New Delhi-110029, Year 1990, Total Pages 240.
Desai, Devangana	:	Moumental Legacy Khajuraho, published by Oxford University Press, YMCA Library Building, Jai Singh Road, New Delhi-110001, Year 2004, Total Pages 107.
Deva, Krishna	:	Temples of Khajuraho, two volumes, published by the Director General, Archaeological Survey of India, Janpath, New Delhi, Year 1990, Total Pages 406 Vol. 1.
District Megistrate, Chhatarpur, M.P., Shri Shukla, O. N.	:	Gazette of District Chhatarpur, M.P.
Deputy Director, Archaeological Survey of India at Khajuraho	:	Rare Books Photographs and documents
Tewari, Ganga Sagar	:	Khajuraho, Itihas aur Murti Shilpa (in Hindi),

published by North-Central and Zonal Cultural Centre, Allahabad, Year 2003, Total Pages 96.

'Vachal' Viswambharnath : Alhakhand published by Shri Durga Pustak Bhandar (Pvt) Ltd., 527 A/2 Kackernagar (Dariabad), Allahabad-3, Year 1986, Total Pages 68.